20

200 Fishing Tips Series

200 CARP TIPS	– Dick Langhenkel Nico de Boer
200 ROD BUILDING TIPS	– Kees Ketting Nico de Boer
200 SEA FISHING TIPS	– Ivan Garay Igor Garay
200 ZANDER TIPS	– Kees Ketting Henk Peeters

200 FISHING TIPS SEA FISHING

IVAN GARAY
IGOR GARAY

Percival Marshall, London

A "Shooting Times and Country Magazine" book, produced by Argus Books Ltd, Watford, on behalf of Percival Marshall Ltd, Burghley Hall, 809-813 High Road, Leytonstone, London E11

ISBN 0 85242 617 8
First published 1982

Cover: John Darling
Photographs: Ivan Garay, Roger Baker and Bruce Vaughan
Sketches: Jaap van der Heide
U.K. editors: Roger Baker and Bruce Vaughan
Translation: Marian Powell

Printed in England by Pindar Print Limited,
Scarborough, North Yorkshire.

CONTENTS

INTRODUCTION

In their efforts to paint a complete picture of the delights of angling – efforts inevitably doomed to failure – the authors of books on fishing only too often lose themselves in a torrent of poetical expression. The present book is designed to avoid the pitfalls of excessive romanticism and with it a lack of practical information. The necessity of summarising a single aspect of sea fishing in a maximum of 15 lines forced us to be concise. In all modesty, the result is a book crammed with information.

The beginner will be guided in his purchase of efficient equipment, but the book will be equally useful to the experienced fisherman looking for wider scope in the field of sea fishing. And fortunately there is plenty of scope!

One example is the development of techniques in fishing for species swimming in the upper levels, for instance shad, mackerel, bass etc, due to the introduction of floats which can be cast over vast distances.

Another flourishing method is fishing with an artificial bait, a method developed when it was found that, in addition to mackerel, nearly all sea fish can be tempted by specially designed streamers and spoons. We are constantly engaged in experiments with artificial baits.

In Holland we were the first to mention the possibilities of catching the mysterious mullet; in Dutch coastal waters these fish grow larger than almost anywhere else in Europe. In this book we shall tell you how to lure this fantastic game fish.

In view of the enormous scope of the subject we were obliged to limit the information on fishing from large and small boats. A subsequent book on boat fishing may follow in due course.

We very much hope that reading the following tips will increase your pleasure in sea fishing still further.

Tight lines!

Igor and Ivan Garay

1. GENERAL

1

Three methods of sea fishing

We can fish from the beach, from jetties, dykes, piers and other coastal reinforcements. In this book these will be combined under the heading "beach fishing".
We can also fish from large boats, chartered by groups of anglers or plying for individuals. We call this "charter-boat fishing".
Thirdly it is possible to fish from small boats, usually holding only two or three anglers. This exciting, but rather dangerous form of sea fishing is referred to as "boat fishing".
Beach fishing is practised by hundreds of thousands of anglers and it is for them that this book is chiefly intended. Sea fishing from small boats is developing rapidly. Many boat fishermen are now organised in clubs, which devote a great deal of attention to the safety aspect.

The cost of beach fishing equipment

Let's be frank: it costs more than you might expect. In beach fishing it is sometimes necessary to cast the bait over a great distance in order to make catches, and this requires good quality equipment, consisting of a strong, long casting rod and a quick-recovery reel. Such things are not cheap. A good casting rod will cost £40 to £50 and a reel will set you back by £30 to £60. In addition you will need line, leads and hooks, say about £10 worth. The minimum cost of essential equipment thus totals £100. Could it not be done for less, "just to try"? No, honestly, it cannot. Inadequate equipment will not yield results and as a consequence you will lose interest. And you will surely agree that unused cheap gear is a pure waste of money.
You should therefore start with good quality equipment. If necessary save up for it a little longer; you will not regret it.

Rods for hire on charter boats

Nevertheless it is possible to become acquainted with sea fishing without a large initial outlay, namely by joining a large charter boat. These generally carry rods for hire. In some places rods can also be hired from local firms. If you have enjoyed your fishing trip you can then buy your own equipment, but we repeat: go for good quality. If you should be one of the few who, after a couple of excursions, do not become addicted for life to this method of fishing, good quality secondhand equipment will always find a ready sale.

The catch of a lifetime: a 15kg (34lb) cod, caught on a 30lb line with a boom and a 1m (three foot) trace. Bait: three lugworms. Location: 3km off Westerschouwen, The Netherlands.

2. RODS

Rod with tip action

Ideal rod with progressive action

Rod too soft or overburdened

Sea casting rod

A powerful casting rod is the most spectacular item of sea fishing equipment. Laymen and freshwater anglers simply do not understand why a sea rod has to be so strong. The importance of a robust rod will become obvious when casting and fishing in a choppy sea on a windy day. The ebb current is so strong that a 150g (5oz) lead will be carried along like a feather. The necessity of a long rod will be clear when a large cod has to be guided among and over shingle.
In enclosed waters very large fish may be caught on relatively lightweight rods. At sea conditions dictate the length and power of the rod, rarely the fish. To console those of you who love the sight of a strongly curved rod: there are opportunities for fishing with light tackle both from boats and from the shore. But for beach fishing the powerful rod is trumps.

Length of a beach rod

A beach rod should be between 3.80 (11ft) and 4.10m (12ft) long. Why these particular limits? Simply because experience has shown them to be suitable for efficient casting and for making fishing a pleasure, much more so than longer or shorter rods. From the technical point of view a 6m (18ft) rod would be even better, but we would be unable to lift such a stick and casting is easiest with a rod of about 4m (12ft). The length of a sea rod plays an important part when dislodging snagged traces, when steering the fish over rubble or when striking a bite. A long rod has the additional advantage of enabling us to mount long traces. The further apart the snoods on the trace, the better. When using a short rod the trace must necessarily be short as well, otherwise it cannot be cast. When purchasing a sea rod these points should be borne in mind.

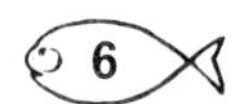

Rod material

Tubular glass – *ie* a tube of glass fibre soaked in polyester – is an ideal material for the manufacture of beach-casters, as it combines light weight with great strength. Heavy solid glass is now quite out of date and we strongly advise you to avoid rods made of this material. Since tubular glass is made in an endless range of quality as well as in a variety of thickness – between 1 and 3.5mm – a beginner will find it very difficult to judge a ready-made sea rod. Even an expert would not find it easy to analyse the properties of a finished rod. The purchase of a casting rod is therefore a question of faith in your dealer, for although a rod costing less than £30 cannot be expected to be of top quality, the price is not a reliable guide.

Action – test curve – strength

Concepts such as action, test-curve and strength play important rôles when the qualities of a rod are judged (see sketch on previous page).
Action is the speed at which a rod straightens after being compressed by the lead during casting.
Test-curve is the curve occurring when the rod is placed under tension. In a sea rod so-called progressive curve is generally to be preferred – *ie* a rod which curves evenly from tip to butt.
Strength indicates the casting weight best suited to the rod; it is experimentally established. This weight subjects the rod to a complete progressive curve and consequently yields the best results. Action and curve can only be judged in practice, or better still, by watching someone else cast with the rod. The casting weight, on the other hand, is now indicated on practically all casting rods.

Two-piece or three-piece rods?

Neither, if only that were possible! A one-piece rod would be greatly preferred, for ferrules and other joints detract from the action of every rod. Unfortunately a one-piece 4m (12ft) casting rod would be practically impossible to transport and the rod is therefore of necessity divided into two or three sections. A two-section rod still measures 2m (6ft), not easy to get into a car. This is why a long sea rod is usually divided into three sections – a concession to the problems of transport regretted by many anglers. Only people who operate from their holiday home or from a caravan can permit themselves the luxury of fishing with a single-piece rod, that is, if they succeed in obtaining an undivided long blank and are prepared to fit out the rod themselves. This is such a simple operation that in our opinion it can hardly be called "rod building".

Ferrules and other connections

The sections of a casting rod can be joined in three different ways. The classical joint consists of brass ferrules. Provided that the female section is reinforced at the rim and midway, this makes a very strong connection. There is also a connection in which two rod sections are joined by means of a spigot made of synthetic material. The two sections do not actually touch, but as the spigot wears out they will come closer. Most factory-made rods have a glass-to-glass joint, in which the sections slide into each other; the female should be reinforced with additional glass fibre. This lightweight but not very robust connection can be reinforced by additional whipping on the female section. Fine fishing line is best suited for the purpose. The whipping is protected by several layers of clear varnish. Nail varnish will do, but special, slow-drying rod varnish is better.

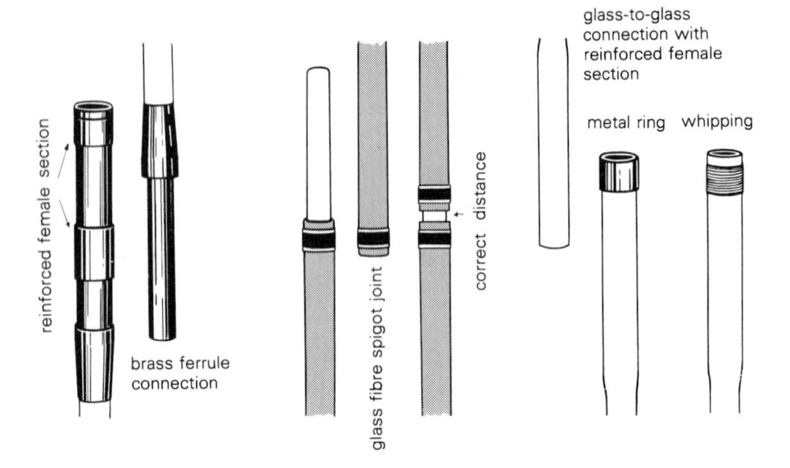

Guide rings

The guide rings serve to transform the spirals released from a fixed-spool reel as quickly as possible into a straight line. To do so efficiently, the butt ring must be slightly smaller than the diameter of the spool. The other rings gradually diminish in size towards the tip ring. The distances between the rings also decrease gradually, so that the thinnest part of the rod carries the largest number of rings. The pressure is thus evenly distributed over the entire rod. In many cases the large butt ring is collapsible or even removable. The guide rings are subjected to great force and must therefore be of excellent quality. Heavy chrome rings are best. This material is guaranteed for wear for two years. Ask for a written guarantee! The popular ceramic or synthetic guide rings will stand up to wear reasonably well, but when the rod is dropped on rocks the ceramic lining may break.

Hand grip, whippings and reel fitting

Without a doubt cork is the best, but at the same time the most expensive material for hand grips. Such handles cost a lot not only because the material itself is expensive, but also because it involves a lot of man hours. The better rods can be recognised by their cork handles. Plastic covered handgrips are extremely strong, but they are cold and slippery to handle.
The ring whippings must be thoroughly protected by several layers of varnish. Extra layers of clear polyurethane varnish are easily added – you can't have too many. The reel seat should hold the reel immovably. A reel seat must be fixed with *two* lock screws. Anodised aluminium is the material most often used, but it has the disadvantage that, when the protective layer is damaged, the aluminium will be affected by seawater. Chromed brass is the best material for reel fittings.

Three ingredients to guarantee a long-distance cast: a strong sea rod, a large sea reel and world champion Ronald Fenger.

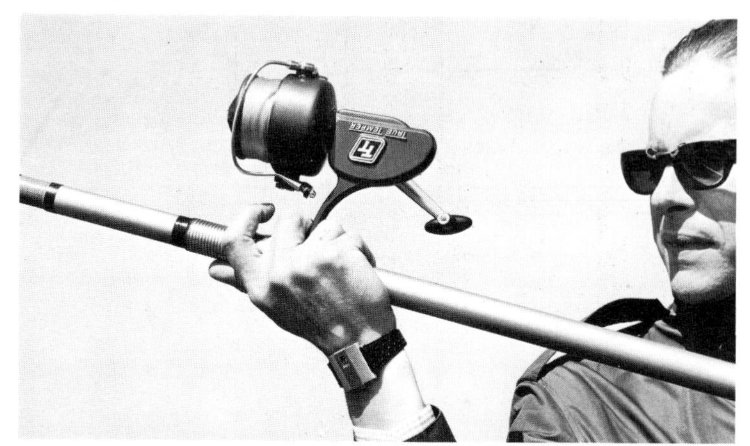

12

Where to buy a sea rod

If at all possible you should buy your rod from a dealer who is himself a sea angler. How to find one? Read *Sea Angling Monthly* magazine and scan the advertisements. A stranger fishing from the shore may put you on the right track, or a telephone call to a local angling club may yield the desired information. Some tackle dealers build their own sea rods. Naturally such rods are more expensive than factory-made equipment, but they are supplied with a longer guarantee, since the maker is bound to back his own product. Possible damage will usually be repaired quickly and cheaply and we therefore regard the extra expense of such a rod fully justified.

Boat rods

At sea we are often forced to fish with leads of 300 grams (10oz) and over and a boat rod must therefore be short and firm. Although solid glass is a suitable material for such rods, we again prefer hollow glass with a wall of adequate thickness. We favour a one-piece boat rod, but if a ferrule joint is used it should be made of reinforced metal.
When fishing for flatfish or eels we use a fairly light rod; cod or ling require a strong rod (20lb or 30lb-class) with a roller tip ring on a firm tip section. That means two separate rods. We solved the problem by making two different tip sections to fit one butt section, a considerable saving in money. You should be able to find a cheap piece of hollow glass. Locating a ferrule to fit the bottom section of the rod may be a little more difficult. The best solution of all is to have a double purpose rod built or to construct it oneself – not really all that difficult.

The demise of a casting rod

A sea rod's robust appearance frequently creates the false illusion that it is indestructible. Nothing is further from the truth, for inexpert handling causes many of these very strong rods to come to an untimely end, usually not in the course of a spectacular battle with an enormous fish, but because the line has caught on some obstacle or other. If this should happen to you, do not wildly jerk the rod, for either the rod or the line will snap. (You will, of course, have tightened the slipping-clutch mechanism of the reel a little). Use the rod as a lever and exert *even* pressure on rod and line. If this does not work you may be able to free the line by walking as far as possible to left or right. If that does not work either, we hold the line in a cloth, pull it taut and again try to free or straighten the hook with a few jerks. Or we take a sad decision and break the line.

3. REELS

Why use a special sea reel?

Well, yes – why? For the simple reason that a freshwater reel is incapable of standing up to very heavy pressure. A sea reel, on the other hand, is of very solid construction. It follows that it is rather heavy, but this presents no problem, as a sea rod is not held in the hand. The material of which the reel is made must stand up to saltwater.
The fast recovery rate of a sea reel is also of the greatest importance, so spare your freshwater reel and leave the heavy work to casting reels constructed for the purpose.

Where to buy a sea reel?

As a price-conscious consumer you might reply: from the cheapest dealer. However, when purchasing a reel you should never be guided by economy alone, for in the course of time a reel will require both maintenance and repair. Maintenance is something you can deal with yourself, but for repairs or the replacement of parts you will have to depend on the dealer from whom you have bought it. Before buying a reel ask whether the dealer can cope with repairs. Many dealers have a stock of spare parts and a repair may be a matter of minutes or at most a few days. If the dealer does not do repairs the reel will have to be returned to the manufacturer, involving you in the expense of postage and delay. Most manufacturers will do their best to save you waiting; some of them repair and return a reel the day they receive it. The following tips refer to fixed-spool reels.

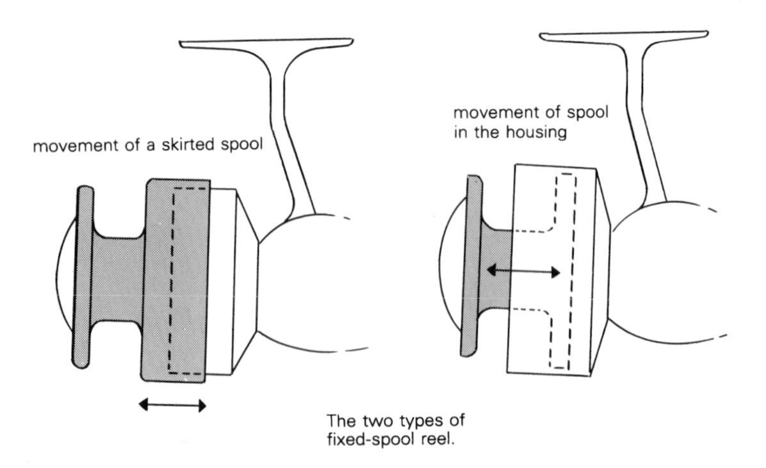

The two types of
fixed-spool reel.

Finger pick-up

If the reel is supplied with a half or full bale-arm, the line is picked up automatically by giving the handle a turn after casting. In the case of a finger pick-up, the line must be caught on your finger after casting and is then transferred to the fixed finger pick-up.
Experience leads us to give you the following advice: always buy a sea reel with finger pick-up, for a bale-arm is a rather delicate mechanism both in use and in transport. A finger pick-up is small and has no moving parts. A reel with finger pick-up is also safer to use, for a bale-arm may close spontaneously during casting, something that is not without danger. Compared to a bale-arm a finger pick-up is more reliable, stronger, cheaper and safer. Despite all these advantages we willingly accept the fact that it is slightly less convenient to use.

Skirted-spool or open spool?

A spool which surrounds the reel casing is called a skirted-spool. If the spool moves inside the housing it is called an open spool.
For sea angling nothing beats a skirted-spool, and for the following reasons.

a. The spool will never be partially inside the housing during casting; this would involve additional friction.
b. The skirted-spool protects the reel against sand. A built-in spool may get jammed by a few grains of sand.
c. In general skirted-spools have a greater diameter than open spools, resulting in a higher recovery speed and less friction during casting.

Some manufacturers now build sea reels incorporating skirted-spools and finger pick-up.

The white Bobynil spool for long-distance casting and the black factory-made deep spool (see tip 20).

Recovery speed

The average angler is able to cast over a distance of about 80m. Proficient casters have no difficulty in covering 100m. We have seen well-known anglers such as Ronald Fenger, John van Hurck and Robert Sebregts cast as far as 170–180m – measured distance.
But, whether it is 80m or 180m, the distance always seems very great when the line has to be retrieved and it is therefore an advantage to have a reel with a high-speed retrieve. Hence we advise the purchase of a reel which winds in 70-90cm (a yard) for each turn of the handle. Higher recovery rates are possible, but in that case the high transmission rate requires so much energy that winding in the smallest flatfish becomes a problem. We are speaking from experience: we once built a reel with a recovery rate of 120cm (four feet) per turn of the handle. Unfortunately it proved quite unusable.

Spools for long-distance casting

20

In their efforts to cover extra long distances, tournament casters like to use specially shaped spools, which enable the line to drop off very rapidly. (It will be obvious that a line dropping from a deep spool will encounter extra friction and with it loss in the distance covered). Since in sea angling it may be necessary to cast over long distances, it seems logical to use long-distance spools in a sea reel as well; the estimated gain in distance covered is about 10–15 per cent. One minor disadvantage of these long-distance spools is the fact that their line capacity is limited; as a rule only a few loops remain on the spool after casting. These long-distance spools, available to fit practically all sea reels, are called "Bobynil long-distance spools" and they are made by Atecom, 48 van Arteveldestraat, B–2000, Antwerp.

Anti-reverse

A reel with an anti-reverse device can be wound forward or backward when the anti-reverse is disengaged.
When winding in a fish one would thus never be able to let go the handle without running the risk that the fish will swim away. We therefore advise you to keep the anti-reverse engaged *at all times*. We entirely disagree with the suggestion that it should be disengaged during fishing, in order to prevent wear and tear.

Spare spool

If you should decide to buy a "Bobynil" long-distance spool, the original spool of your reel can be used as a spare and this is truly indispensable. In your efforts to free a snagged line you may be unlucky enough to lose the entire line and it will be a great advantage if you can immediately fit a loaded spare. Loading an empty or half-empty spool can waste valuable time even if you have plenty of nylon available.
If you own two identical reels only one spare is needed. It is a good idea to tie a shock leader to the line on your spare spool while you are still at home. It is easier to tie an efficient knot in the comfort of your living-room than outside in the cold.

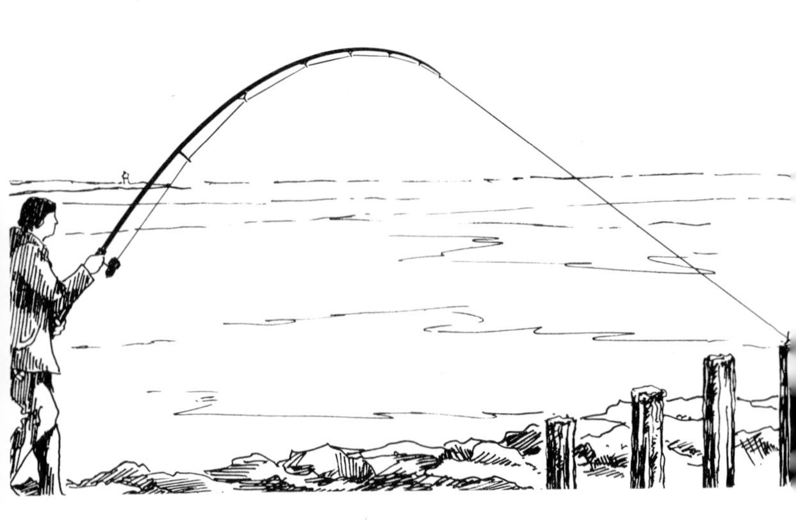

23

Adjusting the slipping-clutch of a sea reel

The slipping-clutch is a kind of safety device. It may prevent the line snapping under excessive strain, for instance when you have hooked a large fish. If the mechanism has been correctly adjusted the line cannot be broken by a strong fish; it will merely be pulled through the slipping-clutch. The correct adjustment of the mechanism is based on the strength of the knotted wet line. The best method is as follows.
One or two of the hooks on your trace are pushed into, say, a wooden post. You now walk back about ten metres. The line is caught behind the pick-up and you continue to walk backwards until you feel the line is fully stretched. The rod is held at an angle of 45 degrees during this operation. The breaking point is reached when there is no more "give" in the line. The slipping clutch is now adjusted by turning the screw, well avoiding the point where the line will break.

Readjusting the slipping-clutch

Right, the slipping-clutch has been perfectly adjusted. However, when line is retrieved it may get caught on an obstacle. To free the line or to straighten the hook you will have to use the maximum strength of your line and to do so, the slipping-clutch must be tightened.
Say you have managed to free the line. In theory you would now have to readjust the mechanism as indicated in tip 23. In practice this is rarely done, for the angler wants to resume fishing straight away. Understandable – but fatal if the catch of a lifetime should suddenly present itself. With a tightened slipping-clutch your chances of landing it would be nil. Hence the following tip: If you should ever have to tighten the screw, count the turns. Afterwards loosen the screw by the same number of turns and the mechanism will once more be correctly adjusted. Some reels incorporate a calibrated dial, which makes the readjustment even simpler.

Maintenance of the slipping-clutch

Although the mechanism is used for long stretches of time in a sandy, salty and damp environment, it is expected to function perfectly at moments when the angler's heart starts to beat faster.
Alas, alas, that is not always the case. The slipping-clutch should therefore be regularly checked and cleaned. Remove the screw, the various braking discs and the spool and clean out all sand and salt crystals. Replace the grease, which is soon affected by salt water. When the mechanism has been reassembled it is once more adjusted as described above. While you are at it, remember to put a drop of oil on the handle, for this is the first part of a sea reel to wear out.

Fixed-spool reel or multiplier?

In the course of time most sea anglers have become so familiar with the use of a fixed-spool reel that they overlook the fantastic opportunities presented by the multiplier. It is often thought that it is too difficult to cast with a multiplier. That is nonsense, for all existing distance records have been achieved with this tool. Unknown is unloved, and the multiplier will therefore never entirely replace the fixed-spool reel, although boat fishermen are well aware of its advantages. As soon as the angler starts to use lines of over 30 lb or weights exceeding 250g (8oz) the fixed-spool reel will rapidly become useless. A multiplier can cope with the thickest lines and the heaviest weights. When you have irreparably ruined your fixed-spool reel you should really try a multiplier. It will prove to be a revelation, for it is by no means as difficult to master as is often thought.

Abu 7000 and 6500c multipliers – ideal for beachcasting.

4. FISHING LINES

27

Reel line

The line loaded on the spool is called the reel line. It must be strong enough to
a. cope with fish you may expect to catch, and
b. deal with the obstacles which may be present in your chosen location.
The first presents few problems; enormous cod (10kgs (20lb) and over) have been caught on 11lb lines. In addition the reel has a slipping mechanism. Nevertheless we sometimes need heavier lines because we often get caught in obstacles, for instance when fishing near rubble deposits or in gullies with clay edges, when brute force must be employed to free the line. The maximum line size in such circumstances is 18lb.
In places where no such obstacles occur the line need not be heavier than 11lb.
Whatever breaking strain line you use inspect it frequently for signs of abrasion caused by the sharp teeth of some species and/or stones and rocks on the sea bed.

Supple or firm?

Fishing lines are made in a variety of grades between supple and firm. So far as the reel line and the trace are concerned it makes no difference which type you choose, but for the short snoods to which the hooks are tied the line can never be too flexible. A biting fish might be alarmed by a stiff snood and reject the bait. You should therefore buy a few reels of the most supple fishing line available. Several manufacturers include such lines in their collections. An 11lb line is suitable for flatfish, and if you intend to fish for codling a length of 20lb line will come in handy. The colour is of no importance. Choose clear line; it is an open secret that chemical dye can only weaken the line.

Line stretch

Every fishing line has a certain percentage of stretch, varying between 15 and 30 per cent. Say your hook snags on an obstacle about 100m from the beach. Before approaching the breaking strain of the line you will have to walk back 15 to 30 metres without rewinding the line. Only then will you be able to exert maximum force on the line.
In sea angling this large amount of stretch is actually undesirable. The less stretch, the better; it is advisable to choose line with little give. As a rule the modern, very expensive, but exceedingly strong fishing lines stretch very little.
If you want a line entirely free from stretch you should buy a braided terylene. This line can only be used in a revolving multiplier.

This exceptionally heavy cod was caught from a boat on an Abu multiplier. Fishing line: 12lb terylene

Kinking line

Kinking is something that is by no means easy to explain. Nevertheless we shall try, for every angler will experience it at one time or another. Take a length of fishing line about 30cm (12in) long. Tie one end to a fixed object and take the other between thumb and index finger. By rolling the line between your fingers you will twist it. This lengthwise distortion is called "kink". If we were to release the line the kink would tend to spring back. If our fishing line should hold a large number of kinks it might suddenly become entangled during a cast, and this will result in line break. While fishing, kinking may occur when you are winding the handle of the reel as a large fish is pulling the line through the clutch. Pay attention to the rattle of a slipping clutch in operation and stop winding when you hear it. A flatfish or eel turning on its axis may also cause kinking.

How to prevent kinking

It is an unfortunate fact that new fishing line, straight from the factory, often has kinks in it. However, we must always make sure that the line does not become even more kinked when it is loaded on the spool. To this effect the factory bobbin must be held in front of the reel in such a way that the spool is wound in the same direction in which the spirals drop off the bobbin.
There are a few simple tricks to get rid of kinking. When fishing from the beach the best method is to cast parallel to the waterline instead of into the water. The rod is then laid down and the lead is removed, after which the line is rewound through a folded cloth. If a lot of kinks are found in the line, stop winding, move the folded cloth along the line to the tip and start again.

This is how the line is wound on to the spool (represented in diagram; in reality the line must of course be kept taut)

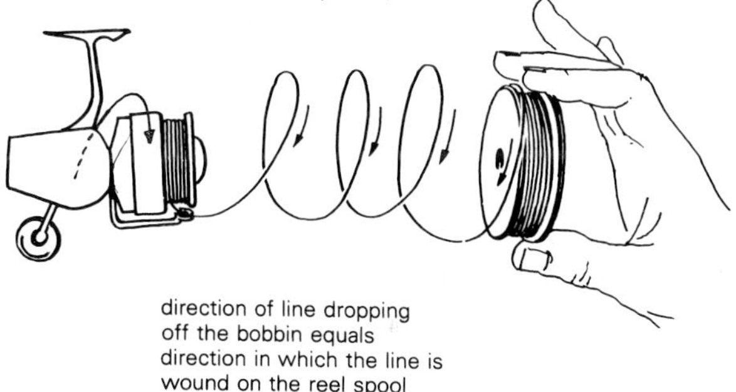

direction of line dropping off the bobbin equals direction in which the line is wound on the reel spool

32

Replacing line

The quality of a fishing line will fairly soon become affected by sunlight. The line will also suffer if it is repeatedly subjected to maximum strain when it has caught on obstacles or when heavy fish are landed. When fishing near submerged breakwaters or from a dam it may moreover suffer mechanical damage.
In short, to avoid unpleasant surprises, which usually occur at inconvenient moments, the fishing line must be renewed regularly. How often?
If you do not fish very often and keep your reel in a dark cupboard, once a year is sufficient. If you fish regularly, twice a year is essential, while fanatical anglers must renew their line at least three times a year.
How much of the line must be renewed? The answer is: the average length of your cast plus 50m; 200m is always right.

33

Economical 1000m bobbins

If (as most sea anglers do) you fish with two rods and you go out regularly, so that the reel lines have to be renewed twice a year, you will need about 700–800m nylon a year; half that amount if you only fish occasionally.
If you buy 100m nylon at a time it will cost you a pretty penny. You might be much better off with one economy spool holding 1000m. Although there is quite a considerable demand for these spools, dealers are not exactly eager to promote their sales; understandably enough, since the profits on the smaller spools are greater. However, you might be able to persuade your dealer to order 1000m spools for you. You need not worry about the quality; as a rule it is the same as that of the expensive smaller bobbins.

34

What is a shock-leader?

The force exerted on the line when 180g (6oz) of lead is cast is so great that the 10lb or 20lb line would inevitably break. To avoid this happening a section of heavier line is tied to the reel line. This is called a shock-leader. The length of the leader is about twice that of the rod, which means that a few loops of the stronger line are wound on the reel before the cast is made. The thickness of the shock-leader is determined by the action of the rod, but especially by the weight of the lead. With weights of 150g (6oz) the shock-leader is in practice never heavier than 40lb. When 125g (4oz) weights are cast a 27lb leader will suffice. Casting technique also plays a part; one sea angler will never have any problem with a given combination (casting rod, weight, leader), while his friend is troubled by breakages when using exactly the same combination. You will have to experiment to find out which shock-leader suits your rod/lead combination.

Constructing a shock-leader

Two reliable knots which can be used to join lengths of nylon of different diameters are the bimini hitch and the double-grinner. As the double-grinner is the easier to tie, we will assume that you are using that one (see tip 63). It is better if you tie on a new leader before each trip – and do it at home. The loose ends should be trimmed very close to the knot and then covered with a tiny globule of varnish. The varnish will keep the knot dry and therefore increase its strength by about ten per cent.
When casting 3–4oz leads you might typically use a 27lb bs shock-leader. For 5–6oz leads we suggest the use of a leader of 40lb bs. The reel line will be, typically, 15lb–18lb bs.
Do not be tempted to use a blood-knot for tying shock-leaders. During the cast the knot may bend and will increase the possibility of the trimmed ends slipping under the turn which traps them. Knots which do not have neatly trimmed ends will pick up weed and jam in the tip ring.
The length of the shock-leader should be approximately twice that of the rod, this will ensure that several turns are on the reel while the cast is being made.

5. HOOKS

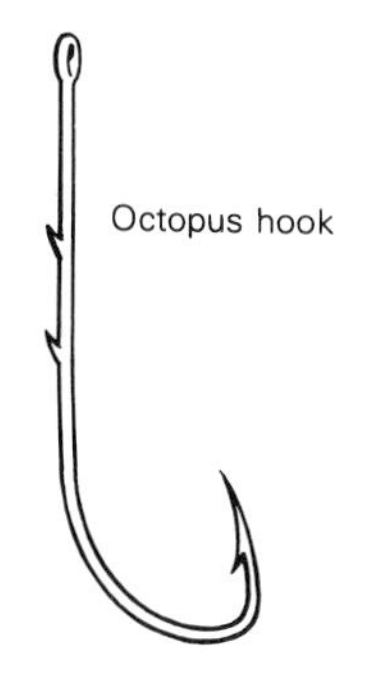

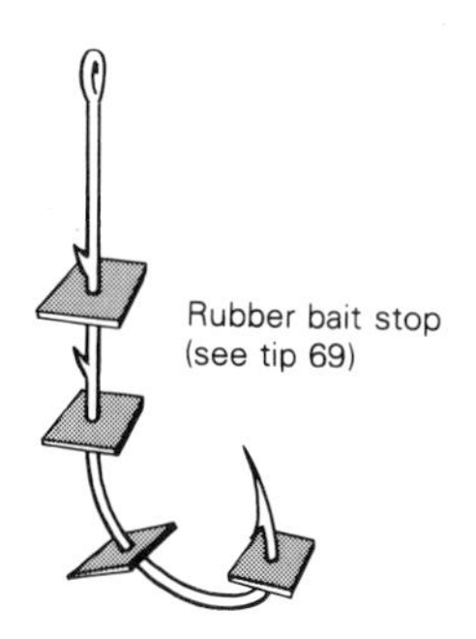

The ideal sea hook

We dutifully try out every hook which appears suitable for sea angling, but we always return to the reliable old Mustad "Octopus". The numerous imitations of this hook vary in quality.
In any case we do not hesitate to call the Octopus the universal hook for sea fishing.
The shank of this hook bears two barbs which prevent the bait (usually lugworm or ragworm) from sliding down. In practice this does not work very well, especially in forceful casts. If it were technically possible the barbs would have to be much longer. The point of the hook is reasonably sharp; only the larger sizes need extra sharpening. The point curves inwards and holds both bait and fish efficiently. A nickel-plated hook can be used throughout the day; after that it will start to rust. This type of hook is suitable for all sea fish, from eels to cod.

Which hook for which fish?

The Octopus hooks described above are made by O. Mustad & Son of Oslo in Norway. The boxes carry the following legend:
Qual. 92247
Hollow Point
Long Point
Mustad Beak Hooks
The size of the hook is indicated in the lower left-hand corner of the box.

Hook size	*Type of fish*
No. 8	Garfish and eels
No. 6	Eels
No. 4	All flatfish and mullet
No. 1	Whiting, codling, bass and mullet
No. 2/0	Codling, cod and bass
No. 4/0	Cod

Storing hooks

Never carry more than 20–25 hooks in your bag or box. Tight-fitting boxes or ring folders (see tip 145) are both suitable for storing hooks. Never put a used hook in the same box or plastic wallet as new ones; they will all rust in no time at all. Hooks kept loose in a box will rub together in transport, with the result that they become blunt. To avoid this happening shake a little greasy talcum powder in the box. We solve the problem by putting a few drops of pilchard oil in the wallet or in the box. The hooks then stick together and remain sharp. The oil also provides protection against rust. Pilchard oil is used to lure the fish and it will therefore do no harm if a little adheres to the hook; the same cannot be said of ordinary oil. Pilchard oil is available practically anywhere. It is sticky when dry and should therefore never be used for rod ferrules or for the reel.

Cheaper by the 100

Sea hooks bought singly or in small quantities are fairly expensive, for you have to pay extra for counting and packaging. Since we emphatically advise you never to use a hook for more than one day, we suggest that you buy your sea hooks in quantities of 100. You will undoubtedly get a discount and the price per hook will be considerably lower than that of hooks bought singly.
Never make the mistake of putting the entire box in your fishing bag or box, for you would be wasting your money instead of saving it. The cardboard box attracts damp and your valuable hooks will rust in no time.
To make sure of getting the same hooks on a subsequent occasion keep the lid of the box bearing the code number. The best method is to buy two boxes at a time and remember to get a replacement when one is empty.

6. LEAD

Lead

If the sombre predictions of EEC economists are to be believed, the world lead supply is rapidly becoming exhausted. Sea anglers greatly contribute to the disappearance of the material: every year tons of it are discarded in the briny! Why lead? The reason is that this material combines high specific gravity with malleability. Lead is moreover (still?) relatively cheap, especially old lead. All these factors combine in making lead the ideal material for the manufacture of casting weights.
Anglers who do a lot of sea fishing may spend a good deal of money on lead. An inquiry among a group of fanatic sea anglers showed that more than half the people questioned made their own sea weights; a remarkably high percentage.

Smooth torpedo leads, resp. 180, 160 and 140g

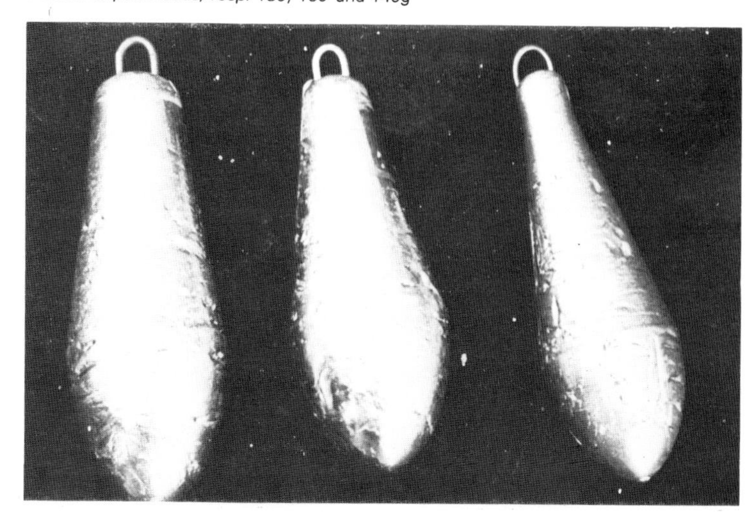

Casting weights

Lighter weights are suitable only in active fishing –*ie* when the rod is held in the hand or the bait is kept constantly on the move. As the tides in our coastal waters create considerable currents and there is usually a good deal of wind, we are often forced to fish with heavy leads. The two most popular weights are 125 and 150g (4oz and 6oz) although we should add that there is a tendency to use even heavier leads. We believe 200g (8oz) to be the maximum. Even with a strong rod a very heavy lead causes sluggish casting. It has the advantage that the bait is held firmly on the hook and that heavy lead is little affected by wind and current. In a gale a heavy lead is essential to get the bait into the water.

The function of lead

The lead weight ensures that the casting rod is put under sufficient tension during casting to transport lead and trace over a great distance. The lead must be of a shape which encounters little resistance during its flight; this means that the centre of gravity should be forward in the lead. Tournament casters will know from experience that tilting lead makes long distance casts impossible. Once the lead has reached the sea bottom it should anchor well, but when line is retrieved the lead must come away easily and not become snagged on obstacles.
As you see, the requirements a lead must meet may be somewhat contradictory. However, a very acceptable compromise is found in the so-called torpedo leads. A torpedo lead is without doubt the best sea lead available. Ignore all other leads (still) available, some of which have the most bizarre shapes.

Casting weight and capacity

Every modern casting rod should bear an indication of its casting capacity. The manufacturer or rod builder has taken the trouble to find out which casting weight gives the best results in combination with a given rod. A rod's capacity provides important information to purchaser and user. Say your rod indicates a casting weight of 150g (5oz). Can you use it with 100g (4oz) as well? Yes indeed, although it will not perform quite as well as with the optimum weight. And what about 200g (8oz)? Most certainly not! If you were to try it your rod would quite possibly crack. A casting rod may be overloaded by at most 10–15 per cent; more than that will lead to rod breakage. If in an emergency you should ever be forced to use too heavy a lead, cast very cautiously, at half strength.

Unacceptable alternative casting weights

Why do anglers sometimes fish in places which are known to be veritable lead graveyards? For the simple reason that there are plenty of fish to be caught in such locations. We know of a location where good codling can be expected. The fact that leads will be lost must be an accepted risk.
If large numbers of weights are regularly lost it may run into a lot of money and it is therefore understandable that ingenious and thrifty people look for alternatives. Numerous strange objects have thus been promoted to casting weights: nuts, bolts, sparking plugs, bicycle chains, etc etc. There is nothing to be said in favour of such misplaced ingenuity. To be frank we consider it deplorable. If the angler wants to economise on lead he should cast his own weights. Please, never tie old iron to your fishing line!

Grip lead

Frequently the current exerts so much pressure on the lead, and especially on the line, that they are driven towards the shore. On an ebbing tide, in particular, there may be such a strong undertow that 20 seconds after a 100m cast lead and trace are almost back on the beach. In a strong current we therefore use the so-called grip leads, ordinary torpedo leads with four metal grapnels. Give this type of lead time to settle after the cast. When the lead has sunk to the bottom start by putting the tip of the rod in the water. After 15 seconds tighten the line and only then lift the rod. In nine out of ten cases the lead will anchor properly.
If you have ever had problems with non-anchoring leads try the method described above. Remember, though, that grapnels will only work well on a sandy bottom.

Four types of grip lead. The two on the right are easy to retrieve because the grapnels are attached to the thickest part of the lead

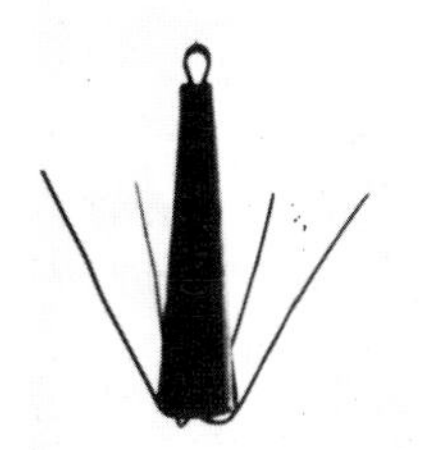

Grip lead or smooth lead?

Since in our opinion grip leads present quite a few problems, we avoid them whenever possible. In the first place grip leads cannot be cast so far as smooth leads, for naturally the spreading grapnels create resistance in the air. Another disadvantage is that grip leads will snag on the slightest obstacle when the line is retrieved. Even on a clean, sandy bottom they will proceed by leaps and bounds. Another disadvantage is the fact that flatfish swimming close to the bottom may be alarmed by the grapnels. We definitely prefer smooth lead. The problem of anchoring lead can often be solved quite simply by using heavier smooth lead. We only resort to grip lead when we are fishing close together with several other anglers and have to avoid our lines getting entangled. Make sure that the grapnels are thin enough, so that they can be straightened by a pull on the line if necessary. (See also Breakaway leads – tip 180).

Leads for boat fishing

When fishing from a large charter boat it is advisable to use the heaviest possible type of grip lead. If you cast it over a large distance (yes, you are reading correctly: casting from a boat) and you manage to anchor the lead, you will be least disturbed by other anglers, nor will you disturb them. If in a strong current grip lead is not used, lead and trace will be carried back to the boat, resulting in monumental tangles with other anglers' traces. When fishing from a small boat casting is unnecessary and ordinary lead can be used, but if several rods are used at once you will have to resort to grip lead for the outer rods. Do not hesitate to use really heavy lead in boat fishing; sometimes 300g (10oz) or more is necessary.

The myth of rolling lead

Some people recommend spherical leads which are supposed to roll along the sea bed, thus covering a large area. Nonsense! It is thought that spherical lead will be rolled along the bottom by the current, but you can take it from us that this is absolutely impossible for the simple reason that the pressure of the current on the line is several times greater than that exerted on the lead. The lead will be pulled in an oblique direction by the line which curves under pressure, and the lead can therefore not roll. No need for regret: towed by the current a lead and the bait on the trace above will cover quite a large area. We never consider it a disaster if our smooth lead is carried some way. In such circumstances we cast a little more frequently in order to remain longer in deep water. A fairly large stretch of water is thus covered, and this never does any harm. Our catches frequently prove it.

7. FLOATS

Casting floats

The recent development of special floats, originally intended only for catching garfish, has made it possible to fish far from the shore for other kinds of fish as well, especially species which occasionally swim at high levels, such as bass, mullet, shad, mackerel and horse mackerel. With these floats, it is even possible to fish for flatfish in shallow water, a very successful method of fishing which is rapidly becoming popular. Even eels can be caught in this way. (If you don't believe us, come and have a look in the creek near West-Kapelle in the Netherlands, where eels are caught solely with floats! Unbelievable but true: with a float five times more eels are caught than by the old method: bait with sliding lead on the sea-bed.)

Long-distance casts

Up to a few years ago the various plastic casting floats available enabled us to cover 30–40m. The insurmountable problem was that because of their lack of stability these floats twisted in flight and tended to spin down. The introduction of the Stabilo float has solved the problem of twisting, with the result that very long casts can now be made. How long? Members of the Rotterdam Casting Club experimented and with a 30g (1oz) casting float achieved 97m (100 yards +) – an incredible distance. The average sea angler should certainly be able to cover 70m and at that distance from the shore there are plenty of fish. Ask your tackle dealer about them.

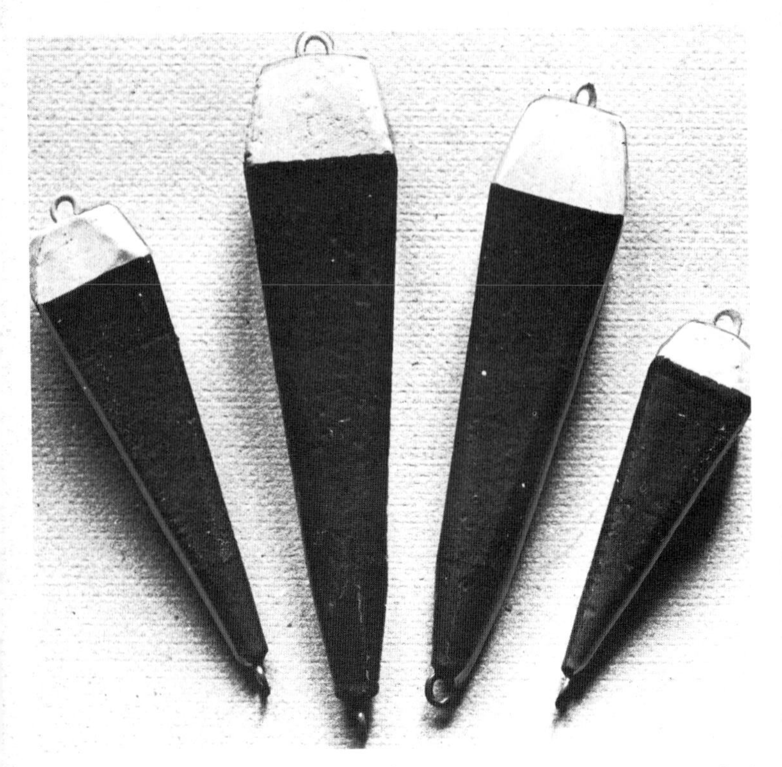

Stabilo casting float in four weights. From l. to r.: 30 (1oz), 70 (2½oz), 50 (2oz) and 15g (½oz)

51

A float for shark fishing

When shark fishing from a boat, very large floats are often used to keep the bait at a certain depth. As special floats for shark fishing are rarely available, the sea angler's ingenuity comes into play.

Objects used as floats include: small plastic balls, empty bottles, inflated balloons, glass floats, pieces of foam rubber, etc etc. The famous shark fishers belonging to EFSA on the other hand swear by the plastic floats which professional fishermen use on their nets. These have the advantage of being very cheap: they can often be picked up on the beach.

8. TRACES AND BOOMS

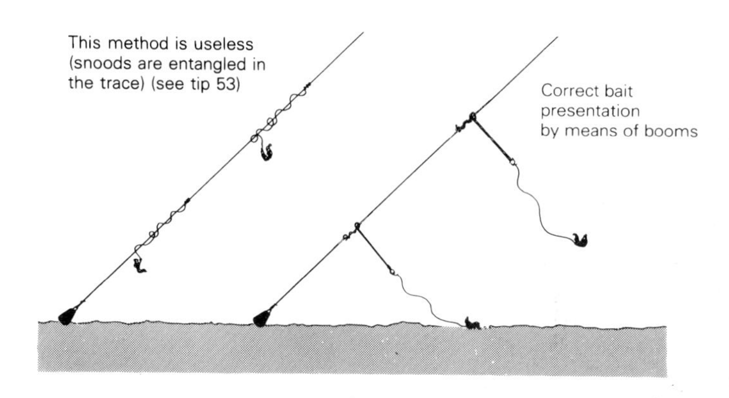

52

The trace

The trace is tied to a swivel knotted to the reel line. It consists of about 1.5m (5ft) of line, to which one, two or three snoods are tied. The hooks are mounted on the snoods. One hook is normally used for codling or bass; for flatfish and eels we generally use two hooks. The snoods should be placed as far apart as possible to cover a large area. When crabs are bothersome we might resort to three hooks, but in normal circumstances a third hook involves unnecessary waste of bait and additional resistance in casting. Sometimes the nuisance of crabs may be largely overcome by regularly winding in the trace a little. Traces are prepared at home. Make a large number, for each trace is used only once. (Discard them at home!) Wrap each trace separately, indicating the type of trace on the wrapping.

Knotted booms

If snoods were to be tied directly to the trace, chances are that they would become entangled during casting. It is unlikely that anything would be caught on these entangled snoods. This is why sea anglers normally use booms, which effectively prevent such entanglements. There are two types of boom: those consisting of heavy knotted fishing line, and metal booms. A knotted boom is made by tying a grinner knot, leaving one end of the line a little longer. The following is another method. The ends of a 10cm (4in) piece of very thick nylon (40lb) are heated, which creates thick lumps. This nylon is passed through a loop of the reel line and the loop is tightened. One lump is held in the loop; a snood is tied to the other end and your boom is ready.

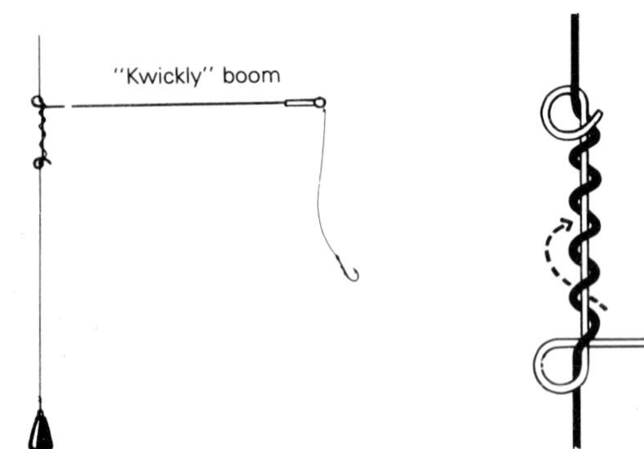

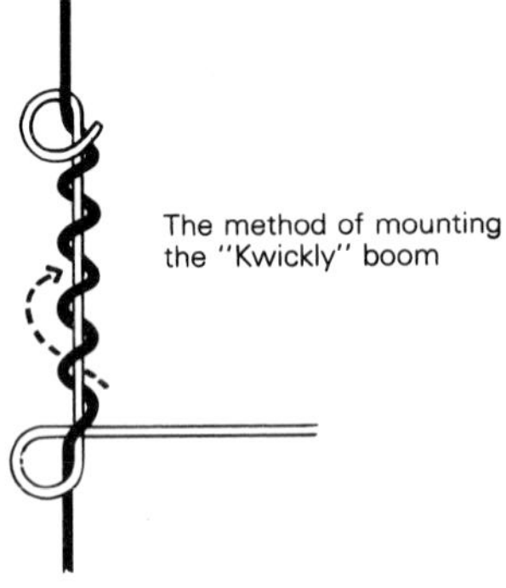

The method of mounting the "Kwickly" boom

Metal booms

The well-known delta boom has the great advantage of being easy to mount and reasonably easy to remove. There are no knots to be tied. A disadvantage is that it is fairly heavy. A great improvement on the existing type has recently been introduced. The "Kwickly" boom (designed by the Dutch angler Jan Clyncke) can be mounted and removed in seconds, without knots. Although it is the same length as the delta boom, far less material is used, so that it is lighter and presents less resistance in casting. We consider it an enormous improvement. The new booms are made in lengths of 12 (4), 22 (8) and 32cm (14in). The snoods must be a little shorter than the boom. These booms are marketed by Albatros BV, Rysenhour, The Netherlands.

The modern "Kwickly" boom between two older, heavier models

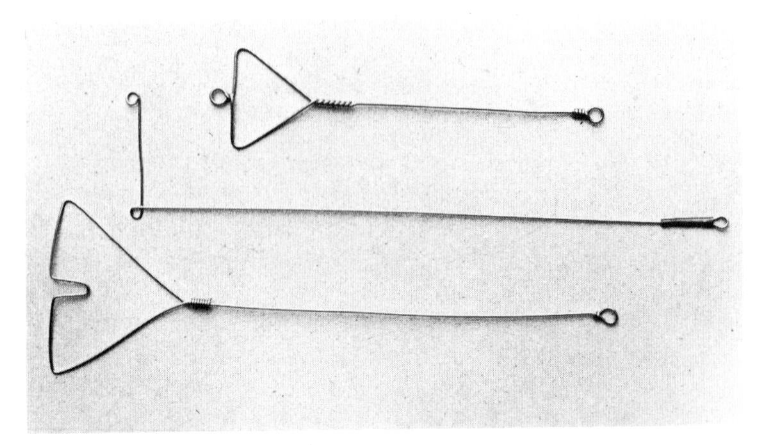

The angled boom

Anglers all over the world use a very cunning device which makes it possible to present the bait close to the bottom (where most fish feed). This is the so-called running boom, which is designed in such a way that the bite is experienced right up to the rod tip. However, this boom used to have one great disadvantage: it could never be longer than 10–12cm (4in), since otherwise the wire would bend under the weight of the lead. This meant that trace and reel line could not be kept far apart. In practice this meant that if the lead were lowered in the normal way, the tackle would often become entangled all the same. Needless to say casting was out of the question. We were so impressed by the enormous advantages of the running-boom system that we racked our brains for a long time to discover how this boom might possibly be improved. We wanted to fish with very long traces of flexible nylon (drift lines) and if possible to cast with a boat rod, in order to fish beside the boat as well as away from it.
After repeated failures we suddenly had the idea of replacing the running boom with a brass tube – and this proved to be the solution. The reel line is passed through a 25cm (10in) length of tubing and the bait can now be lowered without the risk of entanglement. With some care this angled boom can even be cast; to our mind an added advantage.
Although initially we used shorter booms as well, we now restrict ourselves to the 25cm (10in) model, which is much more satisfactory than the shorter boom. Another important advantage is that the lead on the boom can be rapidly changed by means of a spring clip.

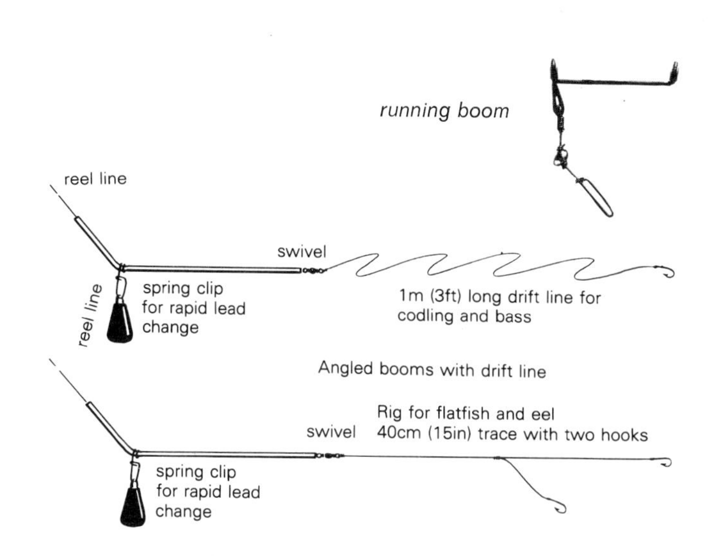

Angled booms with drift line

9. ROD RESTS

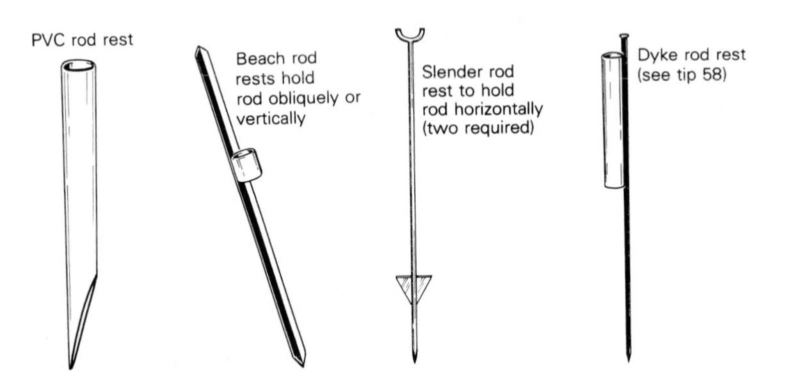

56

Rod rests

Most sea casting rods are too heavy to be held in the hand even for a short period and rod supports are therefore indispensable. When the angler depends on the behaviour of the rod tip to register a bite, the rod should preferably be placed vertically in the rod rest, or alternatively at an angle of 60 degrees. A very firm support is required for this. If the rod is inclined further or placed horizontally at least two rod rests are needed. These need not be quite as robust as the single support mentioned above and are easily constructed.

Rod rest material

If you can afford it, and it is available, choose stainless steel for beach rod rests. If you consider that rod supports made of this material will last for a very long time you may be more willing to accept the initial expense. All other metals have their disadvantages. For practical purposes galvanised iron rod supports are used when fishing from breakwaters; in any case they do not last as they have to be hammered in.
Where metal parts of rod rests may come into contact with the rod we must resort to plastic covers or sections of plastic tubing. Rod rests are frequently left behind and it is therefore advisable to mark them with your name and address.

Beach or breakwater rod rest

It would simplify matters if rod rests were to be suitable both for the beach and for use on groynes, but this is rarely the case. Rod rests used on the beach must have a wide base to present sufficient resistance to the taut line on the vertical rod. Rod rests made of angle iron are very popular.
Less force is exerted on a rod placed horizontally on the rod rests, and in that case slender long rod rests may be used.
A breakwater rod rest has to be secured in the narrow gaps between the stones, which are, moreover, frequently overgrown. Usually the slender pin of such a rod rest has to be hammered into the gaps. The rod rest itself should never be hammered and a good quality support is therefore always welded to a pin.

Inexpensive rod rests

The simpler the better and this applies to the cheapest rod rest we know, one that is completely rust-proof as well as efficient.
We are talking about a rod rest made of a length of thick-walled PVC tubing. Choose one or two sections adapted to the diameter of your rod handles. They should be 50–60cm (2ft) long. The bottom end is cut obliquely; two half-moon-shaped notches are filed in the top end, using a circular or semi-circular file. This extremely inexpensive rod rest can be used to place the rod in a vertical position and, using two of them, the rod can be placed horizontally in the notches.
Our acknowledgements to an old friend who gave us this tip a long time ago.

Boat rod rests

Are you prepared to listen to the well-meant and money-saving advice from two boat anglers who have learnt from bitter experience? We strongly advise against the purchase of special sea rod rests of the type that is fixed to the gunwales of a boat.
We support our boat rods in the following manner. Using a circular file we have simply made notches in the gunwales of our boat. Alternatively the notches can be made in a piece of wood which is then secured in the desired position by means of string, rubber bands or clamps.
On large charter boats rods leaning on the slippery railing sometimes slide down as a result of the pressure exerted on the line by the current. This problem is overcome by tying a piece of string or a cloth round the railing. The skipper will appreciate it if you remove it after use.

10. KNOTS

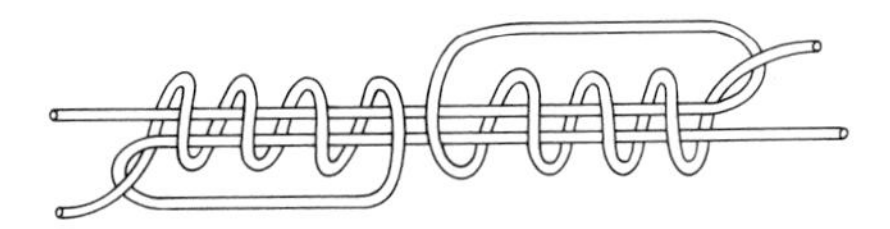

DOUBLE–GRINNER KNOT

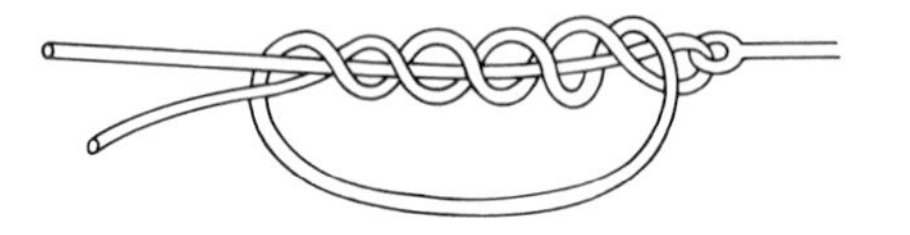

SINGLE–GRINNER KNOT

Three important knots

All knots weaken a fishing line. A bad knot may cause as much as 50 per cent loss in strength, but by using the correct knot the loss may be limited to ten or 15 per cent. And since all lines must inevitably be tied, the use of correct knots is of the greatest importance. A sea angler needs to know only three, but these must be mastered completely. That is why we shall teach you these three knots. Don't be discouraged at the start. The knots may appear somewhat complicated, but you can take our word for it that anyone can learn to tie them.
You should, however, be prepared to practise at home until you are proficient. Practise with ordinary string and change over to fishing line when your knots turn out well. Once you can tie a grinner and a loop knot with your eyes closed you can be satisfied. For the double-grinner you are allowed to keep your eyes open!

62

The grinner knot

This is a very easy knot to tie and one which results in minimal loss of strength. The end of the line is passed through the eye of the hook or swivel and three or four (maximum) turns are made back along the line. With the loose end, form a loop back to the eye. Do not pass the end under the first turn (as in the blood-knot) but make a further three or four turns over the first ones. Now wet the whole lot with saliva then pull both ends in the same direction until all is as tight as it will go. Trim off the loose end with nail cutters.

The double-grinner knot

This important knot is used to connect two lengths of nylon. It is therefore the obvious knot for making a leader, in which lengths of unequal diameter are tied together. When tying a double-grinner knot you will need all your fingers and you will, moreover, have to change over from one hand to the other. The ends are trimmed as short as possible by means of nail cutters. If they are left too long weed will get caught on them. The knot will not be weakened by cutting the ends short.

The loop knot

This is another knot which hardly affects the strength of the line. It is used at either end of a trace. The upper loop connects the trace to a swivel clip on the leader; the lead is connected to the lower loop. It should never be knotted to the trace, for in that case it would be difficult to change the weight. When making a loop knot the loop itself should be drawn gently before end A is pulled to tighten the knot.

Wet knots

Maximum reliability and strength are achieved if all parts of the knot are drawn evenly. In many cases this is impossible because the line has been artificially roughened with resin in the course of manufacture. Fortunately this problem is easily overcome by moistening the knot in your mouth before tightening the ends. If you make a habit of doing so you can be sure of properly drawn knots. By wetting the line before drawing the knot tight, you also ensure that the nylon is not damaged by friction.

11. NATURAL BAIT

66

Lugworm

Lugworms are by far the most popular bait. They are now collected by professional bait diggers on a large scale and the increasing demand can fortunately be met. Fresh lugworms are recognised by their abrupt reaction to shaking or touch. As they go off, the intestines putrefy. Since even fresh lugworms are rather delicate and do not easily remain on the hook during casting, we would advise you to remove the intestines immediately upon purchase. An incision is made behind the head and the inside is pushed out between thumb and forefinger. A lugworm thus treated is hooked very easily and if anything the bait is more efficient in this way. It is a more economical method of fishing. In this form the bait is less easily pulled off the hooks by crabs than are ordinary lugworms and often the worms can be cast repeatedly. If you gut the worms and wrap them in toilet paper and keep them in the refrigerator, they will remain in excellent condition for five or six days.

Ragworm

A ragworm resembles a long centipede and ounce for ounce is reputed to be the most expensive meat available – more expensive than prime steak! It is a very popular bait as it is firm enough to overcome the forces encountered in casting. As ragworms can only be dug up at low tide, the supply varies. Fresh ragworms are rather limp and slimy, but if they are kept in absorbent paper (which must be replaced daily), a great deal of moisture will be lost and the flesh will become nice and firm. Some time before use the worms can be cut into 3 or 4cm (1½in) lengths and wrapped in a cloth or paper tissue. They should be hooked straight across, never through the central intestinal canal. Alternatively whole ragworms can be threaded on to a hook as with lugworms. Be careful when handling a ragworm – it can give you a nasty nip and should never be picked up by the head.

Imported seaworms

Giant sea worms are found on Belgian and French beaches. They are gutted immediately after being dug up and are undoubtedly the most effective bait for catching codling and cod. We suspect that it is the penetrating odour which makes them so irresistible to the fish. At a touch these giant sea worms will contract into a compact little sausage even after three or four days. Deep frozen specimens are also very effective, provided they are fully thawed out. They should be removed from the freezer a few hours before you set out and when thawed must immediately be wrapped in absorbent cloth or paper. Treated in this way they will become reasonably firm and suitable for casting. With the rubber bait stop described in the next tip a boat angler can use recently thawed giant sea worms as well. Ask your local tackle dealer what the chances are of him importing some.

Rubber bait-stops (see sketch preceding tip 36)

In the course of our experiments we were inspired to use small pieces of rubber to hold soft bait more firmly on the hook. The results exceeded all expectations. The 8 x 8mm (half-inch square) bait-stops are cut from fairly thin inner tyre tubes. After mounting a piece of bait a stop is pushed right up against it, preventing it from sliding down. The process is repeated until the hook is effectively baited (for codling). When rebaiting the hook, the rubber stops are simply torn off and discarded. Never use such a bait stop for a second time. They cost nothing, after all, for any garage will be only too pleased to give you an old inner tube. Mussels and other soft bait can be mounted in this way as well as large sea worms from the deep freeze.

Soft crab

At regular intervals the crab's protective shell becomes too small and has to be shed. Until a larger shell has been produced the creature is temporarily a soft crab. A female crab is fertile at this time only; as a rule the situation is underlined by its odour. We suspect that this specific scent attracts fish as well as the crab's mates. All species of fish adore soft crab, which you can find hiding under rocks and weed around the shore during summer. Sometimes hard crab can be useful. If, when the tip of a claw is broken off, a soft grey toe becomes visible, it means that the crab is about to shed its shell. Soft crab can be mounted in one piece, but it may also be cut into smaller sections, which are secured with thread or with a rubber band.

71

Smelts and sprats

Comparative tests have proved that sprats make excellent bait, far exceeding ragworm and lugworm in efficiency. How to obtain this type of bait? Deep-frozen sprats and smelts are available from a number of suppliers, but to make the best use of this bait the sea angler will have to learn how to deal with it. Simply thawing out the bait in the plastic box is not sufficient. Like the imported giant worms, the bait must be thawed out a few hours before a fishing expedition and then wrapped in absorbent material. Treated in this way both smelts and sprats make excellent bait for boat fishing and should not merely be regarded as a substitute when no lugworm is available.

Dead fish bait

Nearly all sea fish are predators and no small fish is safe in the sea. A strip of fish looks and tastes exactly like a small fish, especially in active fishing, and for that reason makes effective bait. Garfish and shad are by no means the only fish which hunt the small fry. If you ever find yourself out of bait you should try pieces of fresh fish. The strips are best cut with a razor-blade or very sharp knife. Before cutting pieces of garfish tail and scales must be removed. The belly of a mackerel provides fine strips. In many countries anglers habitually catch a few mackerel for bait before starting to fish in earnest; in these places lugworm and ragworm are rarely used in boat fishing. When fishing with pieces of fish you are advised to renew the strips at least once every ten minutes. Fresh bait is always to be preferred.

Alternative bait

Practically all fish stomachs are found to contain shrimps, and crushed mussels attract everything that swims. Nevertheless shrimps and mussels are not very popular as bait for the simple reason that they are not easily mounted and are hard to keep on the hook during casting. However, in our opinion many anglers, and boat anglers in particular, are too ready to overlook the opportunities presented by shrimps and mussels. Anglers out for codling, especially, should experiment by adding shrimps and mussels to the lugworm and other baits on their hooks. They will thus economise on expensive bait and we can moreover not imagine a passing codling ignoring such a large and tasty snack. Shrimps are easily (and legally) caught with a shrimping net and mussels can be gathered without difficulty at low tide.

Tinned bait – forget it!

We'll tell you how to get rich quick: discover a method for preserving sea bait without loss of efficiency. To date no-one has been able to do so. We dutifully try out every preserved bait that comes on the market, but the results are always negative. Deep-frozen bait occasionally yields results, but so far as catches are concerned nothing has yet been discovered to beat fresh bait. And what is more, the fresher the better. We must therefore regretfully advise you not to waste your money on preserved bait of any kind. If we should ever discover an effective type of preserved bait we promise you that our shouts of joy will be heard all over Europe.

12. ARTIFICIAL BAIT

Feather paternoster

A feather paternoster, the artificial lure most often used in sea fishing, consists of three to seven feathered hooks connected by means of short links to a thicker trace. The angler makes the feathers flutter to resemble a shoal of small fish. Mackerel, shad, bass, mullet and codling are frequently tempted by the sight. Since most commercially made feather paternosters have serious defects, we suggest that you make your own. This has the advantage that the colours can be adapted to the fish, *eg* red-white for bass and green-white for mullet. It is not a difficult job – anyone can do it, even the legendary person who is all thumbs.

Streamers

A more subtle method of fishing is provided by the use of a single feathered hook, called a "streamer". A streamer can be cast with a firm spinning rod or a fly rod. When fishing with a spinning rod a lightweight lead is mounted 50cm (20in) in front of the streamer, or the streamer is tied to a short sideline attached above the terminal lead. The breaking strain of the main line is 7lb to 11lb. You will realise that a strong mackerel caught on such light tackle will provide quite a spectacle, not to mention bass and mullet. However, these joys are reserved only for the solitary angler who has found a good patch, or who owns a small fishing boat. It is impossible to use such light equipment on a large, crowded charter boat, for three or four fishing lines would immediately become entangled in the current.

Pirks and heavy spoons

The depth of the water and the usually very strong tidal currents necessitate the use of heavy artificial bait. Pirks and heavy spoons are the metal baits most frequently employed. A pirk is a banana-shaped piece of metal fitted with large hooks. It is moved up and down in the water and mainly produces catches of the cod family. Most commercially available sea spoons are too light and we therefore make our own from 2–3mm thick brass. The baited flatfish spoon is a very special lure. When fluttering down, and also when dragged along the bottom, this spoon excites the curiosity of flatfish. Fish attracted by the spoon are caught on the baited hook mounted on a 5cm (2in) line behind the spoon. Very successful in some places. To our great surprise we have also caught many big eels with this spoon. Because of the difficulties in production (they are entirely hand-made) these spoons are not commercially available. You will have to make your own.

Above: a large dab caught on a special flatfish spoon

Jigs

This bait consists of a head made of lead, with a tail of feather's or goat's hair concealing the vicious hook. As the line is connected to an eyelet centred on the head, the hook always points upwards and there is therefore little danger of the jig catching on obstacles. In places where pirks and spoons easily become snagged, a jig is usually quite effective. For sea fishing you should buy or make jigs weighing between 30 (1oz) and 70g (3oz). In a heavy current lighter jigs will not go deep enough. The best colour combination for the tail is red and white in equal proportions. Marabou feathers and the hairs of male goats are best.

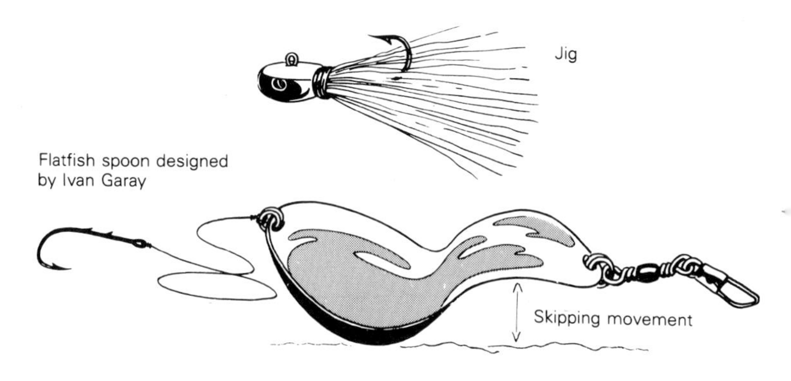

The Redgill – a great bait

79

The Redgill is a plastic imitation of a good-sized sandeel. One's first impression is that this is nothing new – there are plenty of other fish imitators on the market. The special feature of the Redgill is its crosswise tail, which makes it waggle its behind in the most seductive manner! It is said that the Redgill is such an excellent bait that it even provides a living for professional fishermen, who drag it on very long traces and thus catch plenty of bass. Peter Lobs, one-time secretary of EFSA (European Federation of Sea Anglers) sings its praises and taught us how to use it on a fishing expedition in Scottish waters. The lure is tied to a 4m long, 25lb or 35lb trace, which is connected to the reel line via a long angled boom or a long metal boom. A 150g (5oz) lead takes the lot down to the bottom; the line is then slowly wound in. We caught ling, codling, coalfish and pollack with the Redgill – all large specimens.

Below – Two plastic artificial baits, both called a "Redgill". The one discussed in this book is the upper one (imitation sandeel)

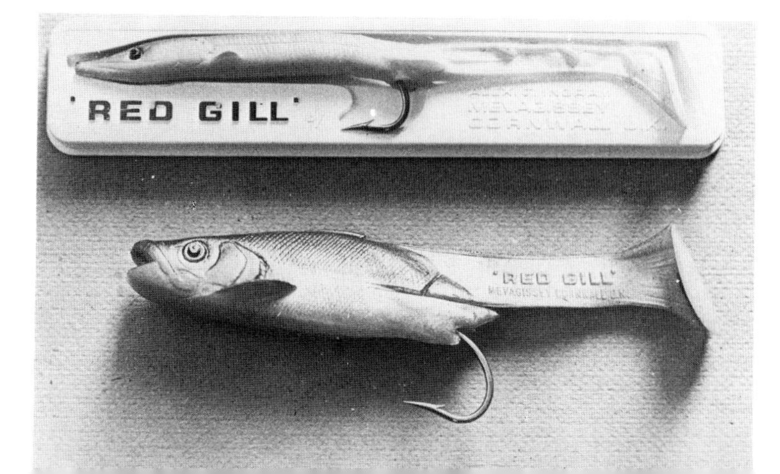

13. STORAGE

The sea angler as a pack-mule

When you see how much equipment a sea angler has to carry you might seriously wonder whether he actually does so of his own free will and for his own pleasure.
What does the equipment consist of? Two heavy sea rods; at least two, possibly four rod rests; two, possibly three large sea reels with matching spare spools; a full bait box; a landing net; lead (always more than is needed); hooks, swivels, booms, spare lines etc etc.
For night fishing a large flashlight or a head lamp with spare batteries is added. On long expeditions food and drink has to be carried as well. It may rain, so rainwear and a large angler's umbrella are also necessary.
And all this gear has to be transported to the fishing patch. Did we hear anyone say: "If they had to do it for a living they'd go on strike"?

The angler's trolley

It would seem that the sea angler's transport and storage problems have come to an end with the introduction of the angler's trolley, the equivalent of the golfer's trolley. We have been testing it for some time and to date our reactions are very favourable. We keep asking ourselves why we never thought before of the possibility of loading all our sea angling gear into a cart. You cannot imagine the relief of not having to carry such burdens. In view of the experiences and reactions of friends we predict a great future for this trolley. What does it look like?
After the wheels have been detached, the wooden body fits in the boot of a family saloon. When the car has been parked, the wheels and the handle are easily fixed and all, literally all, equipment goes into the body of the cart, which is then pulled to its destination. The thick tyres present few problems in loose sand. While fishing we leave all our gear in the cart; there are even supports for our rods. With the change in tides the cart is moved, rods and all. For night fishing a lamp can be fitted, with a battery in the cart. There is a special board for cutting bait. Needless to say there is plenty of room for a folding seat. When it rains the angler's umbrella

is fitted in a special holder. And if you should catch so much fish that you would be unable to carry it, the angler's trolley will provide problem-free transport.
In short, the trolley does everything except fish.
But that is something you will not mind doing yourself.

Seat box

It appears logical that the seat box, so useful and valuable to freshwater anglers, should also serve sea anglers. The box is at one and the same time seat and storage and will hold quite a lot in addition to tackle. What a pity that the popular seat box is unsuitable for use on a wet beach. The wooden frame soon becomes soaked in salt water and both box and contents will deteriorate. We are surprised that there is as yet no waterproof seat box for the sea angler on the market. We truly believe that there is a great demand. As it is, you will have to make your own, as we did. May we give you a tip? Take the size of your car boot into account when deciding on the size of your box. Make it as large as possible. Suitable materials are: waterproof three-ply covered with solid plastic sheets or, better still, with a layer of polyester. For the seat: firm foam rubber covered in PVC.

Plastic seat box

Compared with the wide variety of creels and carrier boxes/seats available to coarse fishermen, you could be forgiven for thinking that the sea angler has had a rough deal from the tackle trade. And you would be right! However, all is not lost. The plastic seat-box, originally designed for match fishermen, has recently been marketed. These boxes are very robust and if you take a walk along a riverbank while a match is in progress you will see anglers sitting on these plastic boxes – often with the bottom half submerged in the water. There are no metal parts so there is nothing the sea can corrode. The lids come equipped with a comfortable vinyl-covered foam cushion.
If you are looking for a seat-box we suggest that you take a look at one of these models.

Fishing bags

The large brown PVC bags are obviously very popular, for more and more anglers are using them. They hold an enormous amount and are easy to carry. The problems arise when they are put down on wet sand. Salt water inevitably gets in through the seams; the results are well-known. Lots of rusty old metal has had to be removed from such bags. We advise their owners to put the bags on a piece of plastic when fishing from the beach. Smaller bags are effectively protected from sand and water by putting them inside plastic rubbish bags.

Tackle boxes

Although sea anglers do use tackle boxes, we must admit that these things are totally unsuitable for shore fishing. On the other hand the box is ideal for boat fishing. You simply put it down at your feet and you'll have everything to hand. We have worn out so many tackle boxes that we can safely say that there are very few good ones on the market. We strongly object to locks bursting open, scattering the contents of the box. Nor do we appreciate it when we find that the box is leaking in a shower. We have once and for all put a stop to these recurring miseries by buying a number of really good quality boxes. They are expensive, but you get what you pay for. On no account take your wife when you go shopping for an expensive make, such as an Umco.

Wooden bait box

In all honesty we must say that the bait boxes on the market are useless for keeping and transporting our expensive bait, for the simple reason that none of them is made of wood, the only suitable material. You will therefore have to make the ideal bait box yourself.
We suggest the following dimensions: 22 x 16 x 12cm (8$\frac{1}{2}$in x 6$\frac{1}{4}$in x 4$\frac{3}{4}$in). Cheap, porous wood is best. Drill 3mm holes in the bottom and in the sides and nail a few 2–3cm (about 1in) slats to the bottom to keep it away from wet sand. The box must be thoroughly rinsed before use, preferably with saltwater. Because the moisture evaporates slowly, the temperature inside the box will remain lower than that of the air outside – just what is needed. The outside of the box is painted white; for night fishing we add a few strips of luminous Scotch-tape. Hinges and the fastener must be made of pure brass.

14. MAINTENANCE

Maintenance of casting rods

In sea angling every piece of equipment has to put up with a great deal of hard use. To avoid our expensive gear having to be written off at an early age as a result of the effects of sand and saltwater, a great deal of attention must be paid to maintenance. The following applies to the casting rod. To prevent sand and salt entering the ferrules it is advisable to join the sections while still by the car. Before doing so the ferrules should be lightly greased. In the absence of a tube or pot of grease a little skin grease (*eg* run the ferrule through your hair) will often suffice.
The rod should also be dismantled away from the shore. Some, usually expensive, sea rods are equipped with ferrule caps – a good idea that deserves imitation. Plastic caps in all possible sizes are generally available for little money. A few spares will come in handy.

Checking the rings

A worn ring can cause a great deal of damage to the expensive fishing line. A damaged line will lose much of its original strength and may rob you of a large fish – adequate reasons for regularly checking the rings for wear and tear. When replacing your fishing line, once a year or more, you should make a point of checking the rings at the same time. Incipient wear is usually clearly visible. Never delay replacement, but immediately fit a new ring.
An old nylon stocking is excellent for checking the rings. When pulled through the eyes it will catch on the slightest roughness. Your wife will be pleased that you are making such grateful use of her old nylons.

89

Maintenance of whippings

The thread with which the rings are whipped to the rod, especially if thin, tends to become loose at the most inconvenient moments. It can therefore only be an advantage to give all whippings extra protection by adding a layer of quick-drying glue, varnish or nail varnish, even in the case of a new rod. We must admit that whipping made of fine thread can be particularly beautiful, but for practical reasons we favour stronger thread. Personally we use ordinary fishing line, not too thin, and as a result we have never had any disagreeable surprises. Carry a roll of sticky tape in your tackle box; it will cope with quite a few mishaps.

Sticking rod sections

Rods fitted with metal ferrules are often difficult to dismantle. This can be prevented by lightly greasing the ferrules before connecting the sections. However, what to do if you find yourself unable to take the rod apart and it will not go into the car? The obvious solution would be to ask someone else to help you, but if two people start pulling away at a rod chances are that something will break. First try warming the ferrules – only at the spot where they stick, otherwise the glue may come off. (Sure, the rod would then be transportable, but you'd have to mend it when you get home.) A little oil may also help. When pulling a rod never hold it by the rings. When someone is helping you, each of you should place one hand above and one below the ferrule.

The rod is beautifully curved by the action of a very large fish. Let's hope the rings are not worn!

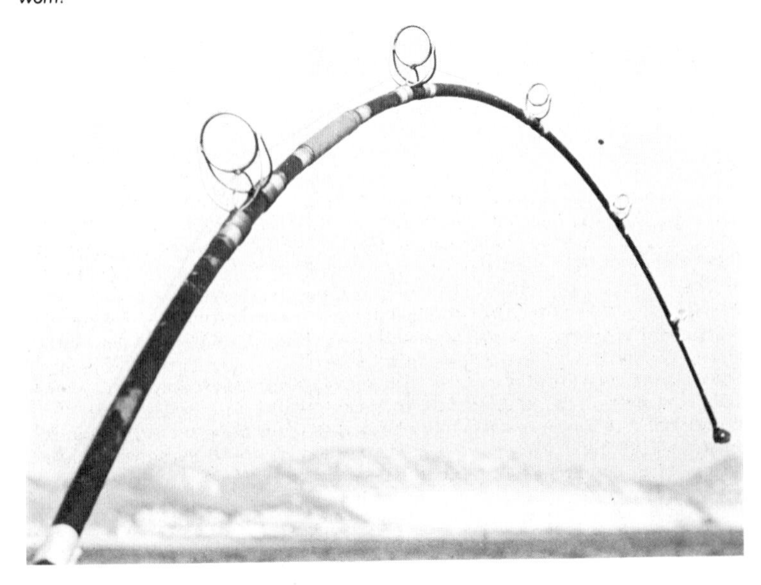

Holes in the cork

Cork is undoubtedly the finest material for rod handles. Only the more expensive rods are now made with cork handles. It is a rather delicate material and at some stage it may become necessary to fill in large or small holes. Larger holes are two-thirds filled with plastic wood. All small holes and the partially filled larger holes are filled with a slow-drying type of glue. The entire handle is then smoothed with very fine sandpaper. Cork dust particles will automatically penetrate the glue. It's as simple as that.

Varnishing a casting rod

For years we treated our rods once or twice a year according to the rules prescribed in various books. This meant that old or damaged varnish had to be scraped off with the utmost care. A tedious job, often involving slight damage to the blank. One day we became so fed up with this task that we resolutely switched over to good quality black car paint. We rubbed down our rods with very fine sandpaper and painted them black. To our great satisfaction we found that the car paint protected the rods far better than thin, delicate varnish. All we have to do is to touch up damaged spots; the annual scraping job is a thing of the past. Why black? Because it provides an effective contrast to the bright beach and also because we happen to like it.

Rod transport

We used to carry our rods in rod bags, but we have now found a better solution. Sand often got into the bags and the canvas or plastic was frequently damp. The bags therefore provided doubtful protection. Rods carried uncovered on the roof-rack of a car at least have the advantage that sand and salt are rinsed off in a shower.

We have found that the PVC tubing available from all DIY shops provides ideal protection for our sea rods. Buy a separate tube for each of your rods – better than one wide one. The tubes are sealed off with plastic caps. Sand or salt are easily rinsed out. These tubes are really ideal and they are moreover cheap. You will undoubtedly find them of great benefit on holiday as well. Fit the tubes with a carrying strap and mark them in several places with your name, address *and* holiday destination.

Reel maintenance

A sea reel is a valuable piece of equipment, which has to function even when dripping with saltwater. After a fishing trip the reel should therefore be carefully rinsed under the tap.
Note: it should be *rinsed*, not soaked or immersed. The reel is then dried. If necessary, grains of sand are removed with a small brush, *eg* a paintbrush or an old toothbrush. All moving outer parts (slipping-clutch, handle, bale-arm) are now oiled with thin oil. Never use thick oil or grease, which will attract sand. Reels with grease nipples must be re-greased with thin grease twice a year. When the nipples are screwed down the grease will automatically be pushed into the bearings.
At least once a year the entire reel must be taken apart and the grease replaced. Thin grease is recommended, otherwise the reel will not function smoothly in winter.

Checking the line

When the line is damaged it is apt to break easily. Line may become damaged in transit if the reel should hit a hard object. Reels should therefore always be wrapped in a cloth or better still, be carried in special reel cases. Line damage may also be caused if the rod falls off the rod rests, especially if it falls on stone or rock.
But most damage is caused by worn-out rings, while in the course of fishing the line may rub on musselbanks or rocks covered in barnacles.
The line can be checked by running it between thumb and forefinger. If any roughness or unevenness is felt the line must be replaced, however disagreeable this may be. If the line feels springy as a result of kinking, it is advisable to do something about it (see tip 30).

15. CLOTHING

96

Arctic or Polar suit

To fish with enjoyment and without danger to your health it is essential for the sea angler to be protected against cold and wind. For this purpose the most important accessory is the so-called Arctic or Polar suit. These suits are worn between underwear and upper clothing and are usually light enough not to impede the angler's movements. The suit traps a layer of air, thus preventing loss of body heat. Thanks to these suits we are now able to fish throughout the year, even from a boat. They are not cheap, but they last a lifetime. As there are unfortunately a number of inferior suits on the market we should like to mention two makes which we have successfully tested, namely those of Abu and Helly Hansen. Most tackle dealers will be able to supply these makes or order them for you.

Boots

The sea angler always has his feet in water and tall boots are therefore indispensable.
Unfortunately it is difficult to keep one's feet warm in these boots. Difficult, but not impossible.
To start with you should buy your boots one and a half or two sizes larger than your normal size in shoes. They must be roomy even when you are wearing two pairs of socks. Yes, two pairs: a pair of thin cotton socks with Norwegian oiled goat's hair socks on top. (They are usually available from shops specialising in ski-wear). If possible both pairs should be knee-length.
If your feet should get chilled in spite of these precautions, wriggle your toes to promote blood circulation, which in turn will increase your body temperature.

Korea boots

In spite of foot exercises the booted boat angler, who in a small boat is forced to sit still for hours on end, will in the course of time inevitably get cold feet. For that reason many anglers change their boots (essential in transit) for other footwear. The ideal alternative is the so-called Korea boot, developed for American troops in Korea. These rubber ankle boots are lined throughout with synthetic fur and are guaranteed to keep the feet warm. There is also a calf-length boot with a detachable fur lining on the market.
We have had experience with both these types of boots and warmly recommend them to boat fishermen, including those who fish from large charter boats. "Deriboots" and "Moonboots" are also very good.

99

Angler's umbrella

Angler's umbrellas are extremely popular among coarse fishermen. They are used in fine weather as well as in the rain and are recognisable from afar. If you ask us, coarse fishermen have a point, for, placed at an angle, the umbrella gives protection from the wind, while upright it keeps off the rain and if necessary the sun.
You can use it to park your wife, sulking or not. A large angler's umbrella can really be very useful to the sea angler when fishing long stints from the beach.
Tip: Carry two tent pegs tied to 3m (9ft) long pieces of string to anchor the umbrella in a strong wind.

Chest or thigh waders

By wearing chest waders or ordinary waders it may be possible to fish quite a long way from the shore, often (but not always) important. Many sea anglers do wear waders. Both have their advantages and their disadvantages. Chest waders enable the angler to wade out farther into the sea. Ordinary waders allow more freedom of movement, but carry a greater risk of wet feet. As chest waders are not ventilated, condensation will occur on the inside and the wearer will quickly get cold. We therefore advise you always to wear an arctic suit underneath.

The Snorkel Parka, the ideal jacket

The very best fishing jacket imaginable, and one by which we have sworn for years, is difficult to describe. We have encountered it under many names; this year ours bear the name "Snorkel Parka". We are so attached to these garments that we always buy two at once, because there have been years when we were unable to find them in the shops. The advantages of these jackets are:

very light in weight
absolutely wind-tight
water-resistant
numerous pockets with closure
the raglan sleeves allow great freedom of movement
warm lining (orange)
sleeves can be tightened at the wrists
zip and button fastening

But the best feature is the enormous hood lined with synthetic fur. The comfort that hood has given us! The price is quite reasonable. Available from many army surplus stores, but usually only infrequently.

Gloves

In the winter the sea angler finds it difficult to protect his hands. True, there are special angler's gloves on the market which leave the tips of the fingers free – including the fingers which are never used, so that the hands get cold anyhow. You'd be better served by a pair of gloves from a surplus store, cutting off the tips of thumbs and forefingers only. The edges must be finished to prevent fraying. Then there is the problem of knitted gloves getting wet. The answer is to wear plastic gloves. Ski gloves bought in the sales are excellent.
Hardy Brothers of Pall Mall have recently launched an absolutely perfect glove on the market. They are made of very supple synthetic leather and have long fingers providing plenty of room. Only the tips of thumb and forefinger are left free. They are lined with foam plastic and we have found them to be absolutely watertight. Their excellence is reflected in the price.

Alaska overall

The very latest in angler's wear is the Alaska overall. This garment is lined from tip to toe and will stop the wind getting at you. In spite of the high price it promises to become extremely popular. We have meanwhile had the opportunity to test the suit and find it eminently satisfactory.
The Alaska overall is, however, not watertight, only water resistant, so take your rainwear when the clouds threaten.

Boot repair

Anyone who can repair a puncture in a bicycle tyre will also be able to mend leaks in rubber boots and waders. When buying a pair of boots always ask for a repair kit. Sometimes it is difficult to locate the leak, but when wet feet give tangible proof that there is one, it must be possible to find it. If it is not immediately visible there are two things one can do.
The boot, filled with air, is held upside down in a bucket of water or in the bath. If that does not work we try another trick. The boot is carefully dried on the outside and is then filled with water.
Mark the leak with a ballpoint pen. Needless to say the boot must be perfectly dry before it is repaired. Most of the moisture will be absorbed by rolled up newspapers.

105

Pocket warmers

There are all sorts of pocket warmers on the market. They create a comfortable warm spot for your hands in the pockets of your jacket. The petrol burning type has a number of disadvantages. It only takes Shell or Esso lighter fuel and lighting it is a delicate indoor operation. In the open air it will usually fail. This warmer moreover spreads a penetrating odour of petrol. The pocket warmer heated by sticks of charcoal has the advantage that if necessary the stick can be lit at either end to make it more effective. Both types will provide warmth for several hours. The very latest type on the market is a warmer activated by . . . a few drops of water; however, the chemical contents only last for fifty hours. Personally we are not very keen on all these gadgets. It is true that they will keep pockets and boots warm, but they are of little use in active fishing.

The ultimate remedy for cold hands

We have frequently had to interrupt our active fishing because our hands were so cold. We are thinking particularly of winter expeditions when we were after cod. Fishing gloves will keep your hands warm for a time, but not in the long run. The uncovered thumbs and forefingers are the first to suffer. We offer you two tried and tested solutions. When your hands are cold through and through, take off your gloves and wrap your hands around a cup of hot tea taken from your thermos. Within a short time the hands will be beautifully warm and the cold stomach will soon recover.
If only your fingers are cold, put them in your mouth for a few seconds. Don't ask us how we got this mad idea, but take our word for it that it works and try it in an emergency.

16. TACKLING UP

107

Tackling up the rod

We have already mentioned that the rod should preferably be assembled away from the beach. Fit the reel in the holder and carefully tighten the lock screw. The rod is now placed on the rod rest in such a way that the entire rod is within reach. Now pick up the line from the spool and pass it through all the rings. If there is a clip swivel at the end of the leader the trace can be attached very quickly. Traces should be prepared at leisure while you are still at home. The lead is attached to the bottom end of the trace either by means of a loop in the main line or better still via a clip swivel. Baiting the hooks is the final operation. You are now ready to cast. Stop! Before you do so position the rod rest(s) so that after casting the rod can be laid down immediately.

Tackling up for float fishing

If anything, tackling up for float fishing is even simpler. After passing the line through the rings, the float is attached by means of the well-known clip swivel. Remember to open the bale-arm if your reel possesses one, otherwise you will be unable to pull the line off the spool. This does not apply in the case of a finger pick-up.
The trace is now connected to the top of the float. Why it should be the top can be read in more detail in the tips on garfish (160–170).
If you wish to fish with artificial bait you can attach anything you like by means of the swivel.

17. CASTING

Learning to cast with a long sea rod

Can casting be learned from a book? We tried it out by giving our non-angling neighbour a casting rod and the two following tips. The results were so encouraging that – with some reservations – we dare give a positive answer to the question. Naturally the angler only becomes proficient in casting by practice, but nevertheless it is possible to learn the principles of the technique without anyone's help. Nevertheless verbal instruction and correction are to be preferred. Some tackle dealers are prepared to *and* capable of teaching you to cast.
Another solution might be to join a casting club. These exist in several places and will be only too pleased to give instruction. The name and address of the secretary of the United Kingdom Surfcasting Federation is Tony Gittins, 21 Peregrine Way, Kessingland, Norfolk.

How to prepare for a cast

Assemble the casting rod and place the reel in the holder on the handle. Pass the line through the intermediate rings and the tip ring and tie a swivel to the end. A safe casting weight consisting of an old nylon stocking filled with 50–60g (2oz) sand and tied at the top is now attached to the swivel. You are now ready to practise casting in a field or on the beach when there is no-one else around. The line is wound in until only one metre remains outside the tip ring. The line is freed from the pick-up and laid on the curved forefinger of the hand which holds the reel. If your reel has a bale-arm it must of course be opened, since otherwise the line cannot leave the spool during casting. Now hold the rod upright and lower the tip behind you until the sandbag just touches the ground. Take two steps forward, slightly dragging the sandbag, and you will be ready for your first cast.

Initiation and progress of a cast

speed up

release line and point rod in the direction of the weight

slowly

The first cast

Slowly move the rod forward over your head. The sandbag will drop to the ground at your feet. It cannot escape since you have not released the line. You now repeat the operation, but when the rod attains the two o'clock position (on a clock face), you allow the line to slip from your finger. There goes the casting weight. Your first cast! Now try gradually to increase the speed at which the rod is moved forward, starting calmly. The faster you move the rod, the farther the weight will be cast. After the line has slipped from your finger point the rod in the direction of the weight (rod at an angle of 45 degrees). Once you achieve some proficiency you can increase the line outside the tip ring (the overhang) to two metres (six feet) and use a slightly heavier weight. In the final step towards perfect casting the weight is not allowed to drop to the ground, but is swung backwards and forwards in a pendulum motion.

Below – How to hold the line when initiating the cast

18. SURVEYING THE PATCH

Surveying unknown patches (1)

If you want to go fishing in unknown water you will avoid a great deal of disappointment by first acquiring as much information as possible. The first step consists of a letter (preferably not a telephone call) to the local tourist information office, with a request for information. Ask for the names, addresses and phone numbers of local angling clubs, tackle dealers, bait sellers, boat hirers and the local harbour-master. Try to obtain further information from one of these addresses by telephone. When you arrive in the place, go to a tackle dealer for verbal information. Dealers are usually well informed, especially if they also sell bait. They will also be able to tell you about boat-hire, but on this subject the harbour-master is an even better source of information. It took us a long time to find out that he is the man who knows literally everything there is to be known about boat-hire and we now always follow his advice, to our great satisfaction.

Surveying unknown patches (2)

It is dangerous to trust blindly in the reports on good fishing patches given in angling publications, even if the details are correct. It is quite possible that hordes of anglers have already congregated at the patch in question. Needless to say the good patch will have been ruined to the bitter fury of the original, and of new, anglers. What you should do is to take a walk along the line of local fishermen who will be in action during the first hours of an incoming tide. A chat with such an angler will do no harm. Start the conversation with a sensible remark about his casting technique or his equipment to show that you are familiar with the subject. Every angler will rightly clam up when asked the stupid question: "Have you caught anything?" No angler should miss the opportunity of watching a fishing match. On these occasions we wear ourselves out plodding past hundreds of anglers, but their catches provide a rich treasure of information.

◁ *A long casting rod – an important item in the sea angler's equipment*

19. BITE REGISTRATION

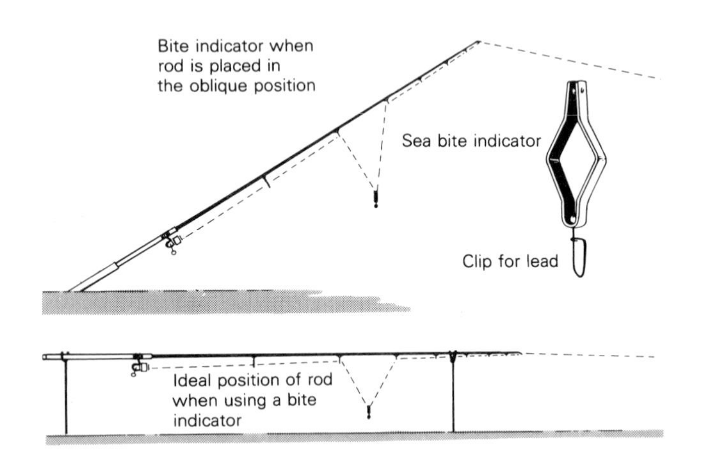

A bite?

To the majority of anglers the moment of the bite is the most exciting of the entire sport. It is therefore strange that most sea anglers fish in a way which makes it practically impossible to see the bite. What happens? After casting, the rod is placed on the rest(s), the line is tightened and the angler gazes intently at the rod tip. A tip which is necessarily fairly thick and stiff, since otherwise it would not serve to cast a heavy lead. Do you really expect a modest bite at a great distance to register on such a thick tip? Possibly – if it is dead calm and the sea smooth. In a strong wind and in surf you will definitely not see a thing. True, the rod tip will move from side to side. Of course it might be a bite . . . but then, it might not. An angler who fishes in this manner does not do himself justice and reduces angling to merely winding in the fish. In the next tip we should like to tell you about a more interesting method.

Fishing with a bite indicator

As a rule very sensitive casting rods are used for carp fishing. Nevertheless you will not find many carp fishers who rely on the movement of the rod tip to register a bite. Usually a sharply reacting bite indicator is chosen; the fish will encounter

little resistance and when the bait is taken the angler can follow the entire process from beginning to end.
Why are bite indicators not used in sea angling? Why not indeed?
Possibly because bite indicators for sea fishing have only recently come on the market, or possibly because a whole series of varying weights would be required.
After some thought and a great deal of experiment we have found a very simple solution. We constructed an indicator with a clip from which any desired lead can be hung. Standard casting leads are used for the purpose.
Rule: The indicator lead must always be 50g (2oz) less than the terminal lead.
This is how the bite indicator is used.
After casting, the rod is placed horizontally on the rod rests. The bite indicator is hung on the line between two intermediate rings. There you are.
Every fish that swims away, but also – and this is something new – every fish moving towards the beach after taking the bait is betrayed by a rising or a dropping of the indicator. The latter occurs very frequently and is rarely visible if one relies on the rod tip to indicate a bite. Even when your attention has momentarily been diverted, the changed position of your indicator will tell you that you have had a bite.
Use a bite indicator wherever practical and your sea angling will acquire a new dimension.

Fishing "by the tip"

If, in spite of our pleas for the bite indicator, you prefer to use the old method, we would advise you to tighten the line after casting until the rod tip is thoroughly curved. Wind and current will have less effect on a taut rod and if the tip is seen to move it might indicate a fish. If you find that the lead comes away as you put the rod under tension, try to anchor the weight by holding the rod tip down. Now release a little line, place the rod in the rod rests and carefully tighten the line. If the lead is torn loose again, either mount a heavier lead or use a grip lead. The latter has the disadvantage that it picks up literally anything in its path.

Alternative bite indicators for sea fishing

If you are unable to find a special bite indicator for sea fishing, you can make do with any other indicator, tying on the indicator lead with string or a hook. In view of the heavy weights involved the indicator clip must be very strong. You could also use a clothes' peg. What should you do when the movement of the bite indicator shows you have a bite? If you are impatient by nature you pick up the rod and strike firmly. The bite indicator will release itself. To avoid losing it, tie the indicator to a tent peg or to a rod rest.
If, on the other hand, you are a cool customer, you calmly approach your rod when a bite is noted, and calmly remove the indicator from the line, putting it in your pocket for the time being. You then pick up the rod and carefully tighten the line. Finally you strike decisively by firmly lifting the rod. To prevent lead and fish becoming snagged you must wind in fast – the faster the better.

20. LANDING THE FISH

Landing nets

Landing nets are rarely, if ever, used in beach fishing. The fact that the lines are relatively heavy in proportion to the fish enables us to drag our catches from shallow water on to the beach. When we have hooked a cod or codling, the fish can be landed with the aid of the surf.
Difficulties arise when we are fishing from a high jetty or breakwater and have to land a heavy fish. It is not possible to lift the fish out of the water by the line. In such cases we usually have to resort to so-called dropnets. These are generally home-made, using an old bicycle wheel as a frame. The often lengthy struggle with the awkward dropnet and with the fish floundering on the surface appears a particularly unsuitable occupation for people with a weak heart.

Landing gaffs

Large fish, such as cod, coalfish and pollack, caught from a boat, will have to be brought in with the aid of a landing net or a gaff.
A landing net often proves to be too small, for a cod may be more than a yard long. And if one is fishing with a feather paternoster, landing a good fish with a net is asking for trouble, for the hooks are bound to get entangled in the mesh. So we'll use a gaff. But the correct handling of a gaff requires a cool head (we are dealing with large fish) and a firm hand – hook the fish in the mouth or in the head. Obviously fish which you intend to return (the majority of your bass for instance) should not be gaffed, but netted or lifted out by hand.

21. SEA FISHING WITH A FLY ROD

Sea fishing with a fly rod

As we are completely obsessed with fly-fishing, we never let an opportunity of using it at sea go by. A fully rigged fly rod is always at hand in our boat and on many occasions it has been bent like a hoop by the furious resistance of a large sea fish. But on innumerable occasions we have had to conclude, to our sorrow, that sea fishing with a fly rod can only be successful when a large number of factors coincide, among others the absence of wind and current and the presence of feeding fish. The current factor alone determines that on any given day we are able to use the fly rod for at most two periods of 15 minutes each.
You will realise that it cannot be done very often, but on the few occasions when we have enjoyed this form of sea fishing we have been so impressed that we intend to continue our efforts. (For equipment see tip 128)

22. NIGHT FISHING

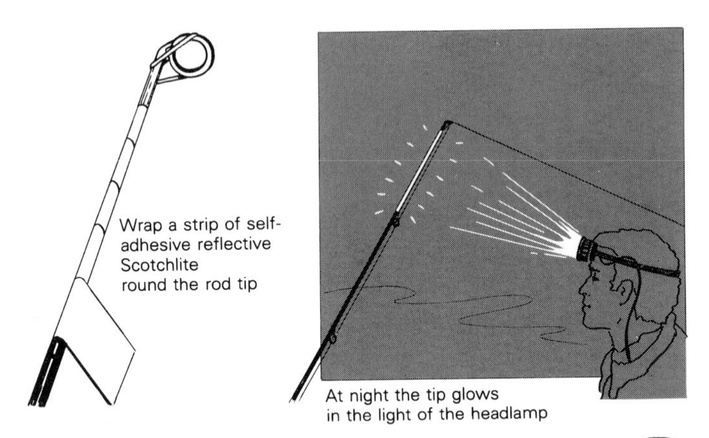

At night the tip glows
in the light of the headlamp

121

Night fishing with plenty of light

A large number of sea anglers are obsessed by night fishing and by no means only because some species, such as cod, eels, and particularly, sole are more easily caught at night than during the day. Of course this is an additional bonus, but we suspect that the very special enchantment of a night spent at sea is possibly the main factor. Is night fishing difficult? No, not much more difficult than fishing by day. This is due to the ingenuity of pioneers among night anglers and also to the invention of the modern high-pressure oil lamp. This extremely expensive lamp is often used in night fishing. Unfortunately it spreads so much light that the user runs the risk of blinding himself as well as his neighbours. We would therefore urge you strongly to mount a reflector cap. As it is very difficult to warm up the lamp on a windy beach, you are advised to light it in the shelter of your car.

Night fishing with a headlamp

Many anglers regard the bright light and the hissing sound of the high-pressure oil lamp as an unacceptable intrusion in the peace and romance of the night. A possible alternative is the use of a headlamp, which lights up the spot towards which the wearer is looking. The use of a headlamp is combined with the application of strips of Scotchlite to the rod tip, the bite indicator and the bait box. These strips are self-adhesive and last a lifetime; they glow clearly in the light of the headlamp. (The same material is used to light up road signs). One advantage of the headlamp is that the angler can never be blinded, because he is always behind the source of the light. There are various efficient and reasonably inexpensive headlamps on the market.

23. BOAT FISHING

123

Fishing from large charter boats

Sea fishing from a large charter boat appears such a simple matter, but it is by no means so. The heavy current and the lack of space make angling quite difficult. In order to keep out of the over-fished area close to the stern of the boat (where everybody else is fishing and where lines frequently become entangled) the bait must be cast a distance. This entails the use of a long beach rod. If in addition a heavy lead is used you might have a chance to catch a fish and not your neighbours! Only the anglers fishing from the stern of the boat can use boat rods, since from that position no casting is necessary. However, the best place is the bow of the boat. From here you will be able to cover a fairly large area without anyone bothering you. To be sure of adequate elbow-room your party should charter the whole boat.

Sea fishing from a small boat

It appears that increasing numbers of sea anglers are realising their long-nurtured dreams of possessing their own boat. The large number of accidents among boat owners fishing at sea indicates the necessity of thorough information about fishing boats and their use. When these accidents are analysed they show that inexperience is the largest danger factor. What are we to say about the cases of drowning which occur every year as a result of the boat capsizing? In many cases the boat has capsized because the anchor was hauled in over the side of the boat. How easily such an accident could be avoided! Always haul the anchor in over the bow. If you are caught in a fog you should only move in the case of extreme necessity and then only provided that you have a good compass and know your course.

Mark the various favourite fishing patches on your map, indicating the course which will take you home in each case. And tell your family or friends where you intend to go fishing and when to expect you back.

Small boat fishing technique

In a small boat casting is unnecessary and short, lightweight rods can therefore be used. In any case it would be impossible to store and handle a long casting rod. Two anglers, each with two rods, will be able to bottom-fish comfortably from a small boat, each with one rod at the stern and one further towards the side. A combination of angled boom or running boom with a trace of flexible nylon will produce the best results.

So much for bottom fishing. Other possibilities for the boat fisherman are: fishing for mackerel and shad with artificial bait, fishing for bass and mullet using a feathered paternoster and the finest, but at the same time the most difficult of all: waylaying all kinds of sea fish with a fly rod. As you see, fishing from a small boat provides by far the most opportunities for all methods of sea angling. Hence its rapid development in recent years.

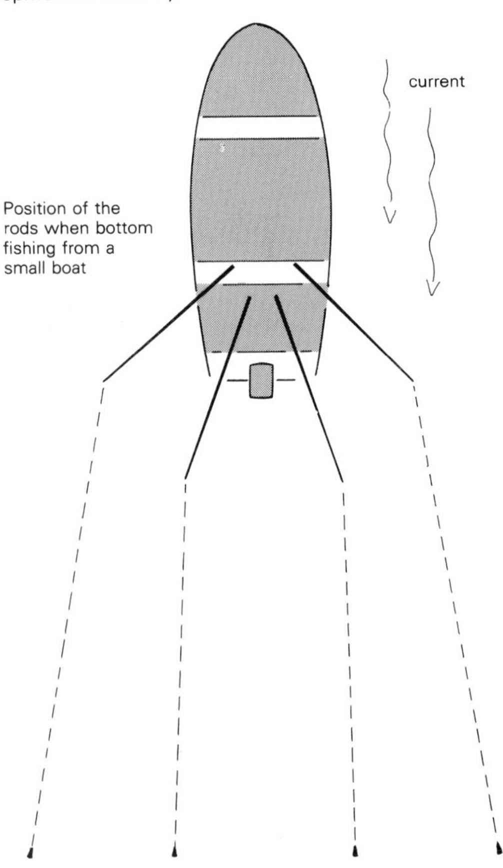

Position of the rods when bottom fishing from a small boat

24. ORDERLY FISHING

126

Orderly fishing (1)

As fellow anglers, may we point out a few moral as well as legal obligations? Yes? Right, here we go. Will you remember to close all gates and barriers through which you have passed? And may we remind you that you should never, never throw away lengths of fishing line? Not on land, not on the beach, nor at sea! A great deal of misery will be avoided if you take the line home to be thrown away there. Needless to say you do not carelessly throw away hooks either, whether baited or not. Take the lot home with you. Keep Britain tidy! Plastic bags are a blessing, used for collecting rubbish. In winter there is no reason why you should not clean your fish on a deserted beach, but when there are people about you must make sure that the trimmings are not left behind on the beach. Bury them, or, from a boat, deposit them far out to sea. Crabs and gulls will make short work of them.

Orderly fishing (2)

We owe our sport to the fish – let us therefore treat them with consideration. Undersize fish should be put back immediately, having been unhooked in a sportsmanlike manner. This is best done with artery forceps. Fish not intended for consumption should also be put back at once. Fish which become badly damaged by handling can sometimes be released by removing the hook while the fish is still in the water. In many cases the hook will be freed by the fish's floundering. Fish intended for consumption must be killed immediately, preferably by hitting it hard between the eyes with a priest.

25. VARIOUS TIPS

A red and white streamer with a weighted body is very useful for the sea angler who likes to experiment

128

The thornback ray

The quietest time of the year for the sea angler is the period between March and May. The cod season has finished and the bass and mullet are yet to begin. A fish which fills this gap is the thornback ray, or roker as it is often referred to.
Thornbacks are most common over muddy or sandy ground covered by a moderate depth of water. They can be caught in deep water, but not in anything like such numbers. Thornbacks are also lazy feeders, preferring to keep clear of the main tidal flow. You need to find a shallowish soft-bottomed area on the edge of a tide run to be sure of catching these fish. They are not a shoal fish, but travel in small groups numbering four or five. Such a group normally comprises one hefty female and a bunch of lesser-sized males. Fish baits seem to be superior to squid or lugworm, but seafish do seem to change their preferences as we move around the coast. Still, our preference would normally be a tail fillet from a herring or mackerel.

Uptide boatcasting

In the shallow waters off Essex, some charter-boat skippers (operating out of the Thames estuary) have popularised a fishing technique known as up-tide boatcasting. Basically it is beachcasting from a boat, anchoring a bait uptide and using the Breakaway lead, (see tip 180).
Here, the emphasis is on sportfishing, taking good fish – cod, bass, stingrays and smoothhounds – on light tackle. Occasionally tope (up to 50lb) are taken on bass rods and 10lb line.
Once the boat reaches the mark, it is anchored from the bow and anglers cast away from the boat, up-tide. A rod with a fairly soft tip needs to be employed so that a bite is registered by the tip straightening. Incidentally, these skippers and their anglers rate the smoothhound as the hardest fighting fish in English waters.

Record fish?

130

Should you be fortunate enough to catch a fish weighing more than the current British record for the species and wish to claim it as a new record, your first course of action should be to preserve the specimen – a freezer is the simplest and most effective answer. The next step is to contact the British Record (rod-caught) Fish Committee, 5 Cowgate, Peterborough, PE1 1LR (Tel: 0733 54084), who will advise you on how to claim and how to go about having the fish inspected and verified by an expert on behalf of the committee. The names and addresses of two reliable witnesses to the capture are required by the committee, though if these are not available you can verify the claim by affidavit.
To prevent your either eating or returning a record fish by mistake, acquaint yourself with the record weights of the species of fish that you are likely to encounter. Alternatively, keep an up-to-date record list in one of your fishing coat pockets. Copies can be obtained from the committee at the above address. Records, at the time of writing, are listed in the next tip.

The British Record (rod-caught) Fish Committee
British Record Sea Fish List
Boat and Shore

131

B = Boat Record S = Shore Record

Species & Scientific Name		Weight					Date	Captor & Location
		lbs	ozs	dms	kilos	gms		
Angler Fish	B	82	12	—	37	533	1977	K. Ponsford, off Mevagissey, Cornwall.
Lophius piscatorius	S	68	2	—	30	899	1967	H. G. T. Legerton, Canvey Island.
Bass	B	18	6	—	8	334	1975	R. G. Slater, off Eddystone Reef.
Dicentrachus labrax	S	18	2	—	8	220	1943	F. C. Borley, Felixstowe.
Black-fish	B	3	10	8	1	658	1972	James Semple, off Heads of Ayr.
Centrolophus niger	S	2	—	—	—	907	Qualifying weight.	
Bluemouth	B	3	2	8	1	431	1976	Anne Lyngholm, Loch Shell, Stornoway, Scotland.
Helicolenus dactylopterus	S	2	—	—	—	907	Qualifying weight.	
Bogue	B	1	10	—	—	737	1975	D. R. Northam, Plymouth, Devon.
Boops boops	S	1	15	4	—	885	1978	S. G. Torode, Pembroke, Guernsey, Channel Islands.
Bream, Black	B	6	14	4	3	125	1977	J. A. Garlick, over wreck off Devon coast.
Spondyliosoma cantharus	S	4	14	4	2	218	1977	R. J. Holloway, off Admiralty Pier, Dover, Kent.
Bream, Gilthead	B	5	—	—	2	268	1978	A. H. Stratton-Knott, off St. Mawes, Cornwall.
Sparus aurata	S	6	15	—	3	146	1977	H. Solomons, Salcombe Estuary, Devon.
Bream, Ray's	B	6	3	13	2	829	1978	L/Cpl. J. Holland, West of Barra Head, Scotland.
Brama brama	S	7	15	12	3	621	1967	G. Walker, Crimdon Beach, Hartlepool.
Bream, Red	B	9	8	12	4	330	1974	B. H. Reynolds, off Mevagissey, Cornwall.
Pagellus bogareveo	S	3	6	8	1	543	1979	D. Poullard, Le Gouffre, Channel Islands.
Brill	B	16	—	—	7	257	1950	A. H. Fisher, Isle of Man.
Scophthalmus rhombus	S	7	7	8	3	386	1980	B.M.K. Fletcher, Guernsey, Channel Islands
Bull Huss	B	21	3	—	9	610	1955	J. Holmes, Looe, Cornwall.
Scyliorhinus stellaris	S	17	15	—	8	136	1977	M. Roberts, Trefusis Point, Flushing, Falmouth, Cornwall.
Catfish	B	15	12	—	7	144	1973	E. Fisher, off Filey, Yorks.
Anarhichas lupus	S	12	12	8	5	797	1978	G. M. Taylor, Stonehaven, Scotland.
Coalfish	B	30	12	—	13	947	1973	A. F. Harris, Eddystone.
Pollachius virens	S	16	8	8	7	497	1977	N. T. Randall, at Rusty Anchor, Plymouth, Devon.
Cod	B	53	—	—	24	039	1972	G. Martin, Start Point, Devon.
Gadus morhua	S	44	8	—	20	183	1966	B. Jones, Toms Point, Barry, Glamorgan, Wales.
Comber	B	1	13	—	—	822	1977	Master B. Phillips, off Mounts Bay, Cornwall.

Serranus cabrilla	S	1	—	—	—	454	Qualifying weight.	
Common Skate	B	226	8	—	102	733	1970	R. S. Macpherson, Duny Voe, Shetland.
Raja batis	S	150	—	—	68	036	Qualifying weight.	
Conger	B	109	6	—	49	609	1976	R. W. Potter, S.E. of Eddystone.
Conger conger	S	67	1	—	30	417	1967	A. W. Lander, at Natural Arch Rock End, Torquay.
Dab	B	2	12	4	1	254	1975	R. Islip, Gairloch, Wester Ross, Scotland.
Limanda limanda	S	2	9	8	1	176	1936	M. L. Watts, Port Talbot, Glamorgan, Wales.
Dogfish, Black-mouthed	B	2	13	8	1	288	1977	J. H. Anderson, N.W. Poll Point, Loch Fyne, Scotland.
Galeus melastomus	S	1	—	—	—	454	Qualifying weight.	
Dogfish, Lesser Spotted	B	4	1	13	1	865	1976	B. J. Solomon, off Newquay, Cornwall.
Scyliorhinus canicula	S	4	8	—	2	040	1969	J. Beattie, off Ayr Pier, Scotland.
Flounder	B	5	11	8	2	593	1956	A. G. L. Cobbledick, Fowey, Cornwall.
Platichthys flesus	S	5	2	0	2	325	1978	W. Stevens, Teigh Estuary, Devon.
Forkbeard, Greater	B	4	11	4	2	133	1969	Miss M. Woodgate, Falmouth Bay, Cornwall.
Phycis blennoides	S	2	—	—	—	907	Qualifying weight.	
Garfish	B	2	13	14	1	300	1971	S. Claeskens, off Newton Ferrers, Devon.
Belone belone	S	2	8	—	1	134	1977	S. Lester, at Pembroke Bay, Guernsey, Channel Islands.
Greater Weaver	B	2	4	—	1	020	1927	P. Ainslie, Brighton, Sussex.
Trachinus draco	S	1	14	11	—	867	1980	N. Hall, St. Agnes, Cornwall
Gurnard, Grey	B	2	7	—	1	105	1976	D. Swinbanks, Caliach Point, Mull, Scotland.
Eutrigla gurnardus	S	1	8	—	—	680	1977	S. Quine, off Peel Breakwater, Isle of Man.
Gurnard, Red	B	5	—	—	2	268	1973	B. D. Critchley, 3 miles off Rhyl, Wales.
Aspitrigla cuculus	S	2	10	11	1	209	1976	D. Johns, Helford River, Glebe Cove, Cornwall.
Gurnard, Streaked	B	1	—	—	—	454	Qualifying weight.	
Trigloporus lastoviza	S	1	6	8	—	637	1971	H. Livingstone Smith, Loch Goil, Firth of Clyde, Scotland.
Gurnard, Yellow or Tubfish	B	11	7	4	5	195	1952	C. W. King, Wallasey.
Trigla lucerna	S	12	3	—	5	528	1976	G. J. Reynolds, Langland Bay, Wales.
Haddock	B	13	11	4	6	215	1978	G. Bones, off Falmouth, Cornwall.
Melanogrammus aeglefinus	S	6	12	—	3	061	1976	G. B. Stevenson, Loch Goil, Scotland.
Haddock, Norway	B	1	13	8	—	836	1975	T. Barrett, 2 miles off Southend-on-Sea, Essex.
Sebostes viviparus	S	1	3	—	—	538	1973	F. P. Fawke, Southend Pier, Essex.
Hake	B	25	5	8	11	494	1962	H. W. Steele, Belfast Lough, N. Ireland.
Merluccius merluccius	S	5	—	—	2	268	Qualifying weight.	
Halibut	B	212	4	—	96	270	1975	J. A. Hewitt, off Dunnet Head, Scotland.
Hippoglossus hippoglossus	S	14	—	—	6	350	Qualifying weight.	
Herring	B	1	1	—	—	481	1973	Brett Barden, off Bexhill-on-Sea, Sussex.
Clupea harengus	S	1	—	—	—	454	Qualifying weight.	
John Dory (St. Peter's fish)	B	11	14	—	5	386	1977	J. Johnson, off Newhaven, E. Sussex.
Zeus faber	S	4	—	—	1	814	Qualifying weight.	
Ling	B	57	2	8	25	924	1975	H. Solomons, off Mevagissey, Cornwall.
Molva molva	S	15	5	11	6	965	1976	P. Sanders, Porthleven Beach, Cornwall.
Lumpsucker	B	6	3	4	2	813	1968	F. Harrison, Redcar, Nth. Yorkshire.
Cyclopterus lumpus	S	14	3	—	6	435	1970	W. J. Burgess, off Felixstowe Beach, Suffolk.
Mackerel	B	5	6	8	2	452	1969	S. Beasley, north of Eddystone Light.
Scomber scombrus	S	4	—	8	1	828	1952	Sqn. Ldr. P. Porter, Breakwater, Peel, Isle of Man.
Megrim	B	3	12	8	1	715	1973	Master Paul Christie, Loch Gairloch, Scotland.
Lepidorhombus whiffiagonis	S	2	—	—	—	907	Qualifying weight.	
Monkfish	B	66	—	—	29	936	1965	C. G. Chalk, Shoreham, Sussex.
Squatina squatina	S	50	—	—	22	679	1974	R. S. Brown, Monknash Beach, Wales.
Mullet, Golden Grey	B	1	9	15	—	735	1978	B. R. Morin, off east coast of Jersey, C.I.
Liza aurata	S	2	10	—	1	190	1976	R. J. Hopkins, Burry Port, Nr. Llanelli, Wales.
Mullet, Red	B	3	8	—	1	587	Qualifying weight.	
Mullus surmuletus	S	3	10	—	1	644	1967	J. E. Martel, Guernsey, C.I.
Mullet, Thick-lipped	B	10	1	—	4	564	1952	P. C. Libby, Portland, Dorset.
Chelon labrosus	S	10	1	4	4	570	1978	R. Gifford, Lagoon Leys, Aberthaw, Glamorgan, Wales.
Mullet, Thin-lipped	B	4	—	—	1	814	Qualifying weight.	
Liza ramada	S	5	11	—	2	579	1975	D. E. Knowles, River Rother, Sussex.

Opah	B	128	—	—	:	58	057	1973	A. R. Blewett, Mounts Bay, Penzance, Cornwall.
Lampris guttatus	S	40	—	—	:	18	143	Qualifying weight.	
Pelamid, (Bonito)	B	8	13	4	:	4	004	1969	J. Pernell, Torbay, Devon.
Sarda sarda	S	4	—	—	:	1	814	Qualifying weight.	
Perch, Dusky	B	28	—	—	:	12	700	1973	D. Cope, off Durlston Head, Dorset.
Epinephelus guaza	S	14	—	—	:	6	350	Qualifying weight.	
Plaice	B	10	3	8	:	4	635	1974	Master H. Gardiner, Longa Sound, Scotland.
Pleuronectes platessa	S	8	1	4	:	3	664	1976	Master N. Mills, East Point, Southend Pier, Essex.
Pollack	B	25	12	—	:	11	680	1980	R. J. Vines, Lyme Bay, Teignmouth, Devon.
Pollachius pollachius	S	16	—	—	:	7	257	1977	B. Raybould, at Portland Bill, Dorset.
Pouting, (Bib, Pout)	B	5	8	—	:	2	494	1969	R. S. Armstrong, off Berry Head.
Trisopterus luscus	S	3	4	—	:	1	474	1978	P. T. Weekes, off Dover Breakwater, Kent.
Ray, Blonde	B	37	12	—	:	17	122	1973	H. T. Pout, off Start Point, Devon.
Raja brachyura	S	28	8	—	:	12	927	1980	P. Aubert, Plemont, Jersey, C.I.
Ray, Bottle-nosed	B	76	—	—	:	34	471	1970	R. Bulpitt, off The Needles, Isle of Wight.
Raja alba	S	30	—	—	:	13	607	Qualifying weight.	
Ray, Cuckoo	B	5	11	—	:	2	579	1975	V. Morrison, off the Causeway Coast, N. Ireland.
Raja naevus	S	4	8	—	:	2	040	Qualifying weight.	
Ray, Eagle	B	52	8	—	:	23	812	1972	R. J. Smith, off Nab Tower, Isle of Wight.
Myliobatis aquila	S	25	—	—	:	11	339	Qualifying weight.	
Ray, Electric	B	96	1	—	:	43	571	1975	N. J. Cowley, off Dodman Point, Cornwall.
Torpedo nobiliana	S	47	8	—	:	21	544	1971	R. J. F. Pearce, from Long Quarry, Torquay, Devon.
Ray, Sandy	B	4	—	—	:	1	814	Qualifying weight.	
Raja circularis	S	4	—	—	:	1	814	Qualifying weight.	
Ray, Small-eyed	B	16	4	—	:	7	370	1973	H. T. Pout, Salcombe, Devon.
Raja microocellata	S	13	8	15	:	6	149	1976	A. Jones, off Trevose Head, Cornwall.
Ray, Spotted	B	6	14	0	:	3	118	1978	H. A. Jamieson, off Causeway Coast, Northern Ireland.
Raja montagui	S	7	12	—	:	3	515	1977	P. R. Dower, in Stoke Beach Area, Plymouth, Devon.
Ray, Sting	B	59	—	—	:	26	761	1952	J. M. Buckley, Clacton, Essex.
Dasyatis pastinaca	S	51	4	—	:	23	245	1975	A. L. Stevens, Sowley Beach, Hampshire.
Ray, Thornback	B	38	—	—	:	17	236	1935	J. Patterson, Rustington, Sussex.
Raja clavata	S	21	—	—	:	9	525	1980	R. Brown, Auchencairn, Kirkcudbright.
Ray, Undulate	B	19	6	13	:	8	811	1970	L. R. Le Page, Herm, Channel Islands.
Raja undulata	S	15	12	9	:	7	158	1979	C. Shales, St. Catherines Breakwater, Jersey, Channel Islands.
Rockling, 3-bearded	B	3	2	—	:	1	417	1976	N. Docksey, off Portland Breakwater, Dorset.
Gaidropsarus vulgaris	S	2	14	8	:	1	318	1976	N. S. Burt, from a cliff at Portland, Dorset.
Rockling, Shore	B	1	—	—	:	—	454	Qualifying weight.	
Gaidropsarus mediterraneus	S	1	1	4	:	—	488	1976	A. Bayes, Gristhorpe, Nr. Scarborough, Yorks.
Salmon, Coho	MINIMUM QUALIFYING WEIGHT TO BE FINALISED FOR BOAT RECORD								
Oncorhynchus kisutch	S	1	8	1	:	—	681	1977	R. J. McCracken, St. Sampsons, Guernsey, Channel Islands.
Sea Scorpion, Short-spined	B	2	3	—	:	—	992	1973	R. Stephenson, Grt. Cumbrae Island, Scotland.
Myoxocephalus scorpius	S	2	2	8	:	—	977	1972	R. W. Tarn, off Roker South Pier, Sunderland
Scad, (Horse Mackerel)	B	3	5	3	:	1	507	1978	M. A. Atkins, at Torbay, Devon.
Trachurus trachurus	S	2	15	4	:	1	339	1980	J. Bidgood, Padstow, North Cornwall.
Shad, Allis	B	3	—	—	:	1	361	Qualifying weight.	
Alosa alosa	S	4	12	7	:	2	166	1977	P. B. Gerrard, off Chesil Beach, Dorset.
Shad, Twaite	B	3	2	—	:	1	417	1949	T. Hayward, Deal, Kent.
Alosa fallax	B	3	2	—	:	1	417	1954	S. Jenkins, Torbay, Devon.
	S	2	12	—	:	1	247	1978	J. W. Martin, at Garlieston, Wigtownshire, S.W. Scotland.
Shark, Blue	B	218	—	—	:	98	878	1959	N. Sutcliffe, Looe, Cornwall.
Prionace glauca	S	75	—	—	:	34	018	Qualifying weight.	
Shark, Mako	B	500	—	—	:	226	786	1971	Mrs. J. M. Yallop, off Eddystone Light.
Isurus oxyrinchus	S	75	—	—	:	34	018	Qualifying weight.	
Shark, Porbeagle	B	465	—	—	:	210	910	1976	J. Potier, off Padstow, Cornwall.
Lamna nasus	S	75	—	—	:	34	018	Qualifying weight.	
Shark, Six-gilled	B	9	8	—	:	4	309	1976	F. E. Beeton, south of Penlee Point, Plymouth, Devon.
Hexanchus griseus									

	S	NO MINIMUM QUALIFYING WEIGHT						
Shark, Thresher	B	295	—	—	133	804	1978	H. J. Aris, at Dunose Head, south of Isle of Wight.
Alopias vulpinus	S	75	—	—	34	018	Qualifying weight.	
Smoothhound, Starry	B	20	15	12	9	520	1978	B. J. Allpress, at Bradwell-on-Sea, Essex.
Mustelus asterias	S	23	2	—	10	488	1972	D. Carpenter, Beach at Bradwell-on-Sea, Essex.
Smoothhound	B	28	—	—	12	700	1969	A. T. Chilvers, Heacham, Norfolk.
Mustelus mustelus	S	14	14	12	6	768	1977	A. J. Peacock, at St. Donats, Glamorgan, Wales.
Sole	B	4	—	—	1	814	Qualifying weight.	
Solea solea	S	4	14	9	2	225	1980	P. Smart, Guernsey, C.I.
Sole, Lemon	B	2	2	—	—	963	1976	J. Gordon, at Loch Goil Head, off Loch Long, Firth of Clyde, Scotland.
Microstomus kitt	S	2	7	11	1	123	1980	W. N. Callister, Douglas, Isle of Man.
Spanish Mackerel	B	1	—	6	—	464	1972	P. Jones, off Guernsey, C.I.
Scomber japonicus	S	1	—	—	—	454	Qualifying weight.	
Spurdog	B	21	3	7	9	622	1977	P. R. Barrett, off Porthleven, Cornwall.
Squalus acanthias	S	16	12	8	7	611	1964	R. Legg, Chesil Beach, Dorset.
Sunfish.	B	108	—	—	48	986	1976	T. F. Sisson, off Saundersfoot, Wales.
Mola mola	S	49	4	—	22	338	1976	M. G. H. Merry, Fisherman's Cove, North Cliffs, Cornwall.
Tadpole-fish	B	—	11	2	—	315	1980	J. McWhirter, Greenock Esplanade, Scotland.
Raniceps raninus	S	1	3	12	—	559	1977	D. A. Higgins, Browns Bay, Whitley Bay, Tyne & Wear.
Tope	B	74	11	—	33	876	1964	A. B. Harries, Caldy Island.
Galeorhinus galeus	S	54	4	—	24	606	1975	D. Hastings, Loch Ryan, Wigtownshire, Scotland.
Torsk	B	12	1	—	5	471	1968	D. Pottinger, Shetland.
Brosme brosme	S	5	—	—	2	268	Qualifying weight.	
Trigger Fish	B	4	9	5	2	077	1975	E. Montacute, Weymouth Bay, Dorset.
Balistes carolinensis	S	4	6	—	1	984	1975	M. J. Blew, Bossington Beach, Somerset.
Tunny	B	851	—	—	385	989	1933	L. Mitchell Henry, Whitby, Yorks.
Thunnus thynnus	S	100	—	—	45	357	Qualifying weight.	
Turbot	B	33	12	—	15	309	1980	R. Simcox, Salcombe, Devon.
Scophthalmus maximus	S	28	8	—	12	926	1973	J. D. Dorling, Dunwich Beach, East Suffolk.
Whiting	B	6	4	—	2	834	1977	S. Dearman, West Bay, Bridport, Dorset.
Merlangius merlangus	S	3	2	—	1	417	1976	C. T. Kochevar, off Dungeness Beach, Kent.
Whiting, Blue (Poutassou)	B	1	12	—	—	793	1977	J. H. Anderson, Loch Fyne, Scotland.
Micromesistius poutassou	S	NO MINIMUM QUALIFYING WEIGHT.						
Witch	B	1	—	—	—	454	Qualifying weight.	
Glyptocephalus cynoglossus	S	1	2	13	—	533	1967	T. J. Barathy, Colwyn Bay, Wales.
Wrasse, Ballan	B	7	13	8	3	556	1978	D. R. Gabe, off Start Point, near Dartmouth, Devon.
Labrus bergylta	S	8	6	6	3	808	1976	R. W. Le Page, Bordeaux Beach, Guernsey, C.I.
Wrasse, Cuckoo	B	2	—	8	—	921	1973	A. M. Foley, off Plymouth, Devon.
Labrus mixtus	S	1	4	8	—	581	1973	R. Newton, Holyhead Breakwater, Wales.
Wreckfish	B	7	10	—	3	458	1974	Cdr. E. St. John Holt, Looe, Cornwall.
Polyprion americanus	S	2	—	—	—	907	Qualifying weight.	

EFSA, U.K. Section

The letters EFSA stand for European Federation of Sea Anglers, an organisation for the study and practice of sea angling in all its forms. The letters NFSA stand for the National Federation of Sea Anglers, an organisation set up to represent sea anglers in this country. The address of the secretary, Bob Page, is 26 Downview Crescent, Uckfield, Sussex, TN22 1UB.

Nail cutters – ideal for cutting fishing line

Modern fishing lines are so hard and smooth that they are difficult to cut with scissors or a knife. It is possible to cut the line with pliers, but never close enough to the knot. If a piece of line sticks out behind the knot, the line dropping off the reel will inevitably get caught behind it in casting. Fortunately there is a cheap and very effective line cutter in the shape of nail cutters, available from any chemist. These cutters have one disadvantage: after a time they will become rusty. Never mind, we simply buy a few at a time and discard the rusty ones. If you use more than one tackle box put a pair of nail cutters in each. Some tackle dealers sell rust-free cutters.

Lie-detector

Some anglers have obviously lost so much credibility in the past that, to prove exceptional catches, they now have to resort to a so-called lie-detector in order to give exact details of length and weight. The lie-detector is a combination of spring balance and retractable metal tape measure. In a moment of weakness we bought such a lie-detector, although regrettably we cannot afford the luxury of exaggeration. It was a very bad bargain. The spring balance under-recorded (!) and the tape measure soon became rusty and unusable. If you want to weigh your catches accurately you will have to invest in a brass spring balance or a set of Avon scales, while a folding wooden ruler or a cotton tape measure will give you the exact length of your fish. But why go to all this trouble? Much better to have a large catch estimated by your best angling mate, who will back you up if necessary!

Baiting needle for use with lugworms

Although personally we swear by gutted lugworms, we feel it our duty to draw your attention to a handy baiting needle used for mounting whole worms. Having passed the needle through the thick part of the worm, the hook is placed in the curve of the needle and, while the fishing line is held taut, the worm is slid intact on to the hook. The lugworm thus remains undamaged. However, if you have cast incorrectly and wind in again immediately afterwards, you will find that the worm is in tatters. For this reason it is better to thread the line *not* on the hook, but immediately above – *ie* on the line. In casting the worm will slide down, but will still be on the hook.
Note: Without exception all baiting needles on the market are too sharp and you should therefore file down the point. The needle should be quite blunt, as otherwise it will pierce the worm's thin skin or your hand.

136

Reducing the drag of the bait during casting

The cost of a baited hook, where commercially-bought lugworm is concerned, works out at between 15p and 20p a time! A simple way to cut down drag during the cast, enabling you to attain those extra yards, also ensures that none of that expensive bait flies off the hook. Though you will no doubt hear of various modifications to this rig, we have to thank Jim Ingledew of Peterborough for the original idea. To use this technique you will have to make your own leads and modify the mould so that a wire stud protrudes from the top of the lead at an angle of 45 degrees. Once the hook has been baited, an elastic band is placed over the bend of the hook and stretched so that it can be held taut by the stud. As the lead hits the water the elastic band will fly off the stud and the trace will be allowed to flow freely. Alternatively, when using a spiked or break-out-type lead, hang the hook on one of the prongs. The baited hook will come away as the lead hits the surface.

RIG TO REDUCE DRAG ON CASTING

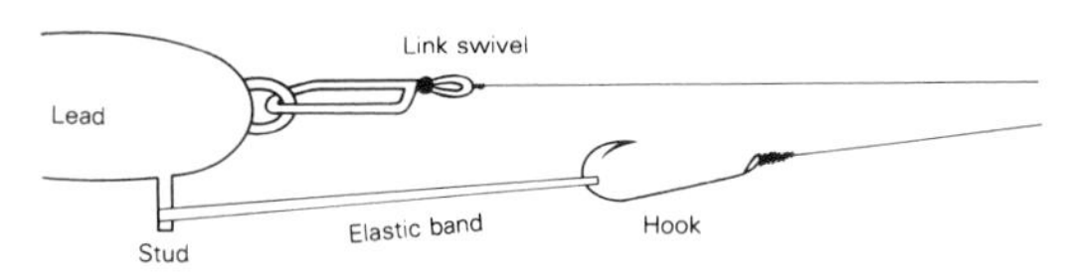

137

Swivels

A swivel consists of two metal eyes which revolve independently of each other. It is a small, but much-used accessory in sea fishing. In principle the swivel is intended to prevent the line kinking, but in this respect it has much less practical effect than is generally thought. If there is a metal clip at one end, the swivel provides a useful aid for connecting objects without having to make knots. Example: attaching an artificial lure to the leader; connecting a trace to the leader; attaching lead to the trace.
You should therefore only buy swivels with clip fasteners. We suggest size five, which is generally applicable. And since you will need a large number, you would be well advised to buy them in bulk.

Clip swivel, an indispensable accessory for the sea angler

Electrical sharpener

Unlike the small sizes of the popular Octopus hook, the larger sizes have to be constantly sharpened. This can of course be done with a carborundum stone, but a better and quicker method is to use an electric sharpener, such as a knife sharpener. At home you can take your time over it. However, be careful never to let the metal get hot, otherwise the hook point will become very brittle. Never hold the hook against the sharpener for more than two seconds at a time; let it get cool in between. You can repeat the operation if necessary. It is a job requiring a lot of patience, but in this way the hooks are made much sharper than with an ordinary carborundum stone. A newly sharpened hook must always be protected against rust. We use pilchard oil for the purpose. (See tip 38).

The indispensable angler's knife

We regard an angler's knife as absolutely indispensable in sea fishing, but we may be prejudiced, for on one occasion we saved our boat from disaster by promptly cutting the anchor rope, thanks to the fact that there was a knife close at hand. Nevertheless a good-quality angler's knife is very useful to the beach angler as well, both for cleaning his fish and for cutting up bait. It can be used to open tins and bottles and in an emergency can be used as a screwdriver. And although a knife is not ideal for cutting fishing line, it can serve the purpose. Make a habit of always putting the knife in the same place after use, otherwise it will get lost in no time. We consider the very thin filleting knives on the market less suitable. Descaling the fish is very difficult with a thin knife. We recommend a strong knife with a sharp point and a blade of 12–15cm (5in).

Minimum sizes for sea fish

Some sea fish are protected by minimum size regulations and undersized specimens have to be put back immediately. They are measured from the tip of the nose to the end of the tail fin. The following species are involved:

Species	Minimum Size	
	Centimetres	Inches
Bass	26	10.25
Cod	30	11.8
Haddock	27	10.6
Hake	30	11.8
Plaice	25	9.8
Witches	28	11.0
Lemon Sole	25	9.8
Sole	24	9.4
Turbot	30	11.8
Brill	30	11.8
Megrim	25	9.8
Whiting	25	9.8
Dab	15	5.9

Since turbot are now rarely caught by anglers, 25cm is practically always safe in the case of flatfish. However, better than adhere to the legal limits, use your own commonsense. Your own limits will undoubtedly be higher than the legal ones, which are really only there to protect the species from the greed of commercial interests.

Paintbrush to the rescue

Many modern rods have glass-to-glass connections or spigot joints.
These connections have the disadvantage that a few grains of sand can create the greatest problems. Either the rod sections no longer fit, or the friction caused by the sand causes damage to the polyester walls of the joint.
We offer a simple solution: we always carry a small, firm paintbrush with which the sand is carefully removed.

Towel

A sea angler constantly has wet hands. Or dirty hands. Or hands that are both wet and dirty. Or hands covered in sand. To fish well you must be comfortable so always take a towel. At home we have a permanent claim on all worn towels and sheets. The sheets are cut into disposable cloths used in eel fishing and unfit for the laundry. Dirty towels are soaked in a bucket of pre-wash solution before going into the washing machine with the rest of the laundry. Remember that the pre-wash is very important. It removes fish scales and we speak from experience when we tell you that mullet scales will effectively put every washing machine out of order.

Cameras and cinecameras

Every sea angler who wants to record his fishing trip on film must remember that sand and salt are a camera's arch enemies. It follows that the valuable apparatus must be very carefully protected. If you have no special case for it, wrap it in a clean towel before putting it in a plastic bag, which should preferably be sealed. Before starting to film or take photographs you must carefully dry your hands.
A word about light adjustment. On a sunny beach there is always the risk of over-exposure, however carefully the apparatus has been adjusted. With a miniature camera, with 36 exposures per film, a shot more or less matters little and every subject should be taken three times – first with the exposure indicated by the lightmeter and the second and third at greater speed or with a smaller aperture.

What have we forgotten today?

Has it ever happened to you that, after a long and exhausting trek to a distant beach you discovered that you had forgotten to bring your bait? Or that you had reached a perfect patch and anchored the boat, only to find that the rods, tackle and all, were still leaning against the caravan on dry land? You can be sure that it has happened to us! Forgetfulness is a human defect. In the excitement of departure a vital piece of equipment is easily forgotten.
We have done away with the problem once and for all by making a check list both for beach fishing and for boat fishing. Before setting out we check all our gear against the appropriate list.
You will now rarely hear us swear when, or rather, before, we are fishing.

Storage tip

In sea fishing it is essential to keep hooks and everything else that can rust, perfectly dry, otherwise these things will be unusable by the time they are needed. If everything is put in separate lidded boxes, the equipment is difficult to find; of course it is always the wrong box that is opened. A fellow angler solved the storage problem by buying a plastic ring-binder, eg 22 x 16cm (available from stationers). This will hold 20 plastic wallets. Holes are made with a perforator. In these transparent wallets everything can be kept dry and clearly arranged: hooks, swivels, streamers, nylon and wire traces, mackerel paternosters and other small accessories. A truly ideal solution which will soon pay for itself, quite apart from the convenience. You will thus be able to see at a glance whether everything needed is present. We are so impressed by the idea that we have filled a separate folder for each species of fish. Very practical!

Disgorging

In a current a feeding fish will usually have to react quickly to take the bait. The fish has to bite immediately, otherwise the bait will have disappeared. This is why in many cases a sea fish will be found to have swallowed the hook very deeply. Since the fish is usually intended for consumption, it should in such a case be killed immediately by a sharp blow on the head. The hook can then be removed at leisure. Artery forceps are the best tool for the purpose.
Actually these forceps should be obligatory.

Artery forceps – the ideal tool for disgorging fish

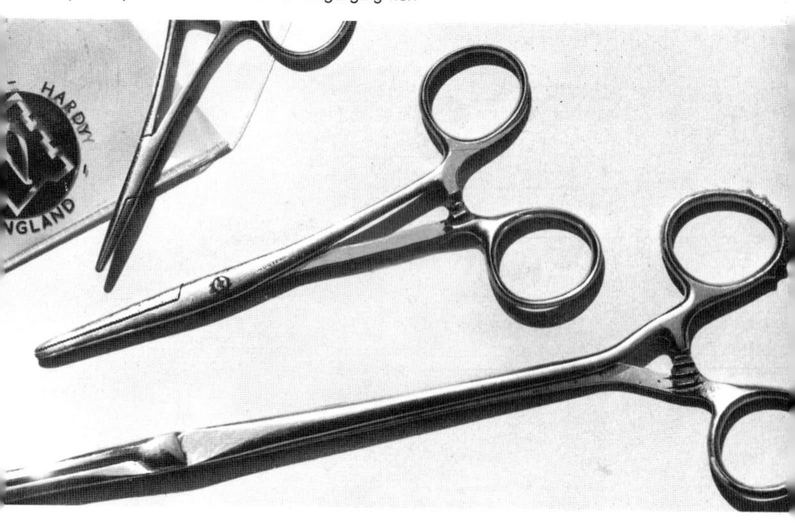

The weather

Boat anglers, especially those who fish from small boats, should keep informed about the weather both before and during a fishing expedition. You can take a small radio on board on two conditions: a) that you use it only to listen discreetly to the weather forecast and do not spoil the environment by music, and b) that the radio is never kept near the compass, which would be affected by it.

Take care

When there is a possibility of strong wind or fog, keep close to the shore and make a note of the course to be set should poor visibility force you to get home by compass. Beware of an approaching thunderstorm. Remember how unpleasant it is to see the lightning strike all around you when your boat is the highest point over a wide area. Also remember whenever you venture out in a boat to inform someone (preferably the coast-guard) of your plans including your estimated time of arrival.

26. FLATFISH

Four flatfish

The flatfish most frequently caught with a rod are the flounder, plaice, dab and sole.
Flounders can be caught practically throughout the year, sometimes in quite shallow water. Plaice, on the other hand, prefer deep water and are caught in coastal waters only at certain times of the year. The dab is another seasonal fish (winter and spring) and must be sought in relatively deep water. Sole like warm water and are caught in late summer/early autumn.
In addition to these four species there are turbot, brill, lemon sole and many other species of flatfish which closely resemble each other. Compared to the four species mentioned above they only occur on a few occasions and consequently are of little interest to the average angler.

How to distinguish flatfish

At first glance all flatfish look alike. How do you distinguish between them? We shall try to indicate the differences. Your own forefinger, moved along the fish from tail to head and vice versa, is the best guide.
Flounder. This dark brown fish is characterised by a number of hard, rough nodules close behind the head. Sometimes they are invisible, but if you feel them, you can be sure that you are dealing with a flounder.
Plaice. The plaice is a very smooth fish in whatever direction it is stroked. It has striking orange spots on the back.
Dab. The dab is pale brown in colour and looks somewhat transparent. When stroking the fish from head to tail it feels smooth, but rubbed the other way the skin is rough.
Sole. Compared to the other three, the sole is clearly different in shape (oval) and is further recognised by its skin, which feels like sandpaper in all directions.

Active fishing

Flatfish often lie impassively on the sea bottom, only taking a bait close to them. When out for flatfish the angler would therefore do well to move his bait frequently. After casting, the trace and lead should be wound in a couple of metres every minute. In this way a larger area of the sea bottom will be covered. If the bait is left in one place, only moving flatfish will be caught. Since you never know when the fish are moving about or are lying under the sand, the active method of fishing will always present better opportunities. Another way is to fish actively with one rod and inactively with the other. You will soon discover which method yields the best results on that particular day. A third method of active fishing consists of holding the rod in the hand and slowly retrieving the line. This is an attractive method. But use a light sea rod, for a heavy rod will constantly become heavier.

Where to fish

Flounder often cause great consternation during angling matches. While the cracks are risking a hernia in their efforts to reach the horizon, women and boys may carry off the prizes with large flounders caught in knee-deep water.
Flounders, especially the very large specimens, like to swim with the rising tide, and by casting too far out one may draw a blank.
On the other hand plaice and dab love deep water and are rarely, if ever, caught in the shallows. In this case the axiom is: the farther the cast the better. The sole is a typical night-feeder and only becomes active after sunset. In the dark this fish will often move to relatively shallow water, while to catch a sole in the daytime it will be necessary to fish the bait in deep water.
As soles and eels like a very muddy bottom, eels are a well-known bonus for the angler out for sole.

Traces

The paternoster is the most popular trace in fishing for flatfish. It consists of a line with terminal lead and two, sometimes three, sidelines. To prevent the snoods getting entangled in the trace it is usual to employ metal or thick nylon booms. It is possible to fish selectively by using very large hooks (no. 4). When smaller hooks are mounted you will often be bothered by undersized flatfish. A successful variant on the paternoster method is created by tying the bottom snood to the eye of the lead. The distance between the snoods will thus be greater, increasing the chance of catching. If the sea bottom is clear an angled boom might in fact be mounted at the bottom end of the trace. The second sideline is attached well away.

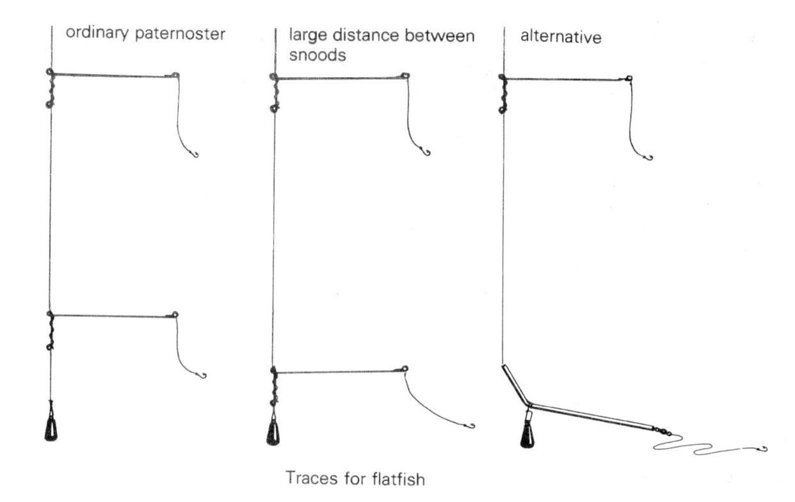

Traces for flatfish

Flatfish special

154

It is well-known that flounders and dab, but especially the former, can successfully be caught with artificial bait. The flatfish is curious about everything that moves within its field of vision and will react by swimming towards the object. Usually it does not bite immediately. The fish first investigates the object and will not bite unless it discovers something edible. It must therefore be lured with artificial bait and must then be presented with a recognisable food item. This is done by tying a short length of line to the spoon or pirk. A small piece of lugworm, ragworm or fish is mounted on the hook and makes the "flatfish special". The baited spoon is allowed to sink to the bottom and is then retrieved about 30cm (a foot) every ten seconds. This involves approximately one turn of the reel handle at a time.
In some places this is the most attractive method imaginable. Except, of course, for the fly rod . . .

27. EELS

Eel grounds

In autumn, when eels are migrating, they can be caught everywhere at sea. But to catch eels throughout the year (with the exception of winter) you will have to choose your patch with care. From personal experience and from our conversations with divers we know that eels tend to stick to one particular place. In lee waters, where sediment is deposited on the bottom, thick layers of very soft mud will be created. It is in such places that eels congregate; sometimes there are as many as 20 per square metre! By fishing in these muddy patches one's chances of a good catch are considerably increased. But there is no guarantee, for there are times when the eel refuses a bait right in front of its nose. An amateur diver, who is also an enthusiastic boat angler, told us that he will make excellent catches one day and draw a blank next day in patches which on a dive he has found to be crawling with eels. It appears to have something to do with air pressure, but it is impossible to be sure when eels will feel like feeding. However, it is certain that eels are much more active at night than during the daytime.

Eel traces

Wading in shallow water, we have often been able to observe the behaviour of feeding eels. Each time the same thing happened when the eel took the bait: the fish vigorously shook its head while swimming backwards. Only then was the bait swallowed. The lesson is obvious: when the fish takes the bait it must feel the least possible resistance, otherwise the bait will immediately be rejected. For that reason long, fine lines must be used in eel fishing. We have tested this theory on many occasions; each time long snoods proved to yield far better catches than short ones. However, in eel fishing the best way to present the bait is by means of an angled or running boom with a very long bait line (see tip 55). And the very best bait for eel is a slightly smelly ragworm. True! Mount the bait on a small Octopus hook, no. 6 or 8, for the eel's mouth is very small.

Eel fishing in practice

In eel fishing the angler is faced with a dilemma with each bite: to strike immediately or to wait a moment? If the former is chosen, chances are that the fish becomes alarmed when the bait is pulled, and will reject it at once. On the other hand, if you wait a moment too long, the hooked eel will have time to twist your trace into a slimy tangle. What to do in such a case?
This is what we do. After a bite we wait ten seconds and then very cautiously wind in about a metre. If resistance is felt we strike at once; if not, we leave the bait where it is, for an eel is often prepared to take a suddenly moving bait for a second time.

Unhooking the eel

To land an eel is one thing, but to unhook the slippery fish is quite a different matter. It happens only too often that an eel, when picked up, slides backwards out of the angler's grasp, in passing catching the unfortunate man's hand on the hook protruding from the mouth. Quite a sight: angler and fish united on one hook! Anyhow, unless you want to make your mates convulse with laughter, you will straightaway wrap every eel caught, including – in fact, especially – the tail, in a cloth or newspaper. It will then not be difficult to remove the hook. Better still, kill the eel quickly and cleanly before attempting to remove the hook. If the hook is caught far back in the mouth do not hesitate to cut the snood and tie on a new one. When out for eel always carry plenty of traces and snoods. And before we forget: a cloth covered in eel slime cannot be washed – it will wreck any washing machine. Use a disposable cloth – but do not discard it in the water or on the shore.

This photograph shows a conger eel next to an ordinary eel. Note the size of the eyes

Conger eels

Normally, very large conger eels are found in deep water, their habitat often being marked by the location of a wreck. Charter-boat skippers are well aware of the exact location of these wrecks and anchor their boats directly over them. The usual method of fishing is to lower fish baits on short boat-rods coupled with heavy leads.

Conger, albeit smaller specimens, can be found close in along rocky shorelines. Where these exist, they can be caught on normal beachcasting outfits. A friend of ours found great sport fishing for conger with standard pike tackle in a Scottish sea loch close to a breaker's yard. He took many eels to 19lb on mackerel dead-baits fished on 11lb line.

Normally, the eels we catch in estuaries are the ordinary freshwater variety or silver eel as it is sometimes called. These can be present in such numbers that they become a nuisance when fishing for other species.

28. GARFISH

Garfish about

Every year in May large shoals of spawning garfish move into coastal waters. Numerous anglers welcome their arrival, because fishing for these slender fish has a very special attraction. Perhaps this is because this exotic-looking fish can be caught with very light tackle, or because the prelude to the bite is usually clearly visible and consequently creates great tension and excitement. Or perhaps it is because the furious resistance of a hooked garfish is frequently accompanied by spectacular leaps? Or maybe it is the challenge because on difficult days a garfish can only be tempted by using exceptionally sophisticated techniques and can only be reached by extra long distance casting?
Whatever the reason, fishing for garfish is a fascinating branch of the sport, provided the correct equipment is used. There is no pleasure in catching garfish on a heavy casting rod, dragging the defenceless fish out of the water on excessively heavy tackle.

A garfish has a narrow, beak-like mouth in which the hook does not easily find a hold

Suitable rods for garfish

A special garfish rod has to meet somewhat conflicting requirements.
1. It must be 3.60 to 4m (10–12ft) long, so that long traces can be used. This will also make it possible to set the hook properly.
2. A garfish rod must have a casting capacity of about 40g (1½oz) and must be capable of casting large floats a long distance.
3. In fishing for garfish the rod is held the whole time and must therefore be as light as possible.
4. On the other hand the rod must be strong enough to lift a garfish weighing several pounds out of the water.
5. The guide rings must be of excellent quality.
All of these features are to be found in an Avon or light carp rod.

162

The Abu 505 – an ideal reel for garfish

Over the years we have used many lightweight reels when fishing for garfish. Several of these "guinea-pigs" have succumbed in the salty environment, especially the extra-light reels, in which the spindle usually became twisted. However, one has survived all our tests, namely the Abu 505. This Swedish reel is very convenient to use and will stand up to heavy loads. Sand and salt will not affect it in any way. The 505 has a closed-face spool and covers equally large distances as a conventional spool. Preparations for casting are childishly simple: when the spool is touched with the index finger the line automatically slips on to it and you are ready to cast. The slipping-clutch mechanism can be adjusted by means of a star-shaped screw. If you notice something wrong while you are playing the fish, the tension can be released in a flash by turning the handle back. Thanks to this facility we have safely landed many a large bass unexpectedly caught on a 7lb line.

The Abu 505 – an ideal reel for the garfish angler

Which line for garfish?

We recommend a 7lb line, since it is capable of casting a 30g (1½oz) float without a leader. This line weight will moreover enable you to lift a large garfish out of the water. When there is no need to cast over a great distance and when the fish does not have to be lifted on the line (*eg* when boat fishing), you could change over to a 5lb line. If you are forced to cast 50–70g (2–3oz) floats you will have to tie a leader to the reel line to avoid the risk of losing your float (see tip 34). For a 50g (2oz) float use a 10lb or 12lb leader; for a 70g (3oz) float the leader should be as much as 18lb. As we are distance fishing with relatively fine nylon, the line may stretch and we therefore recommend the purchase of non-stretch line. The modern super-strong lines all have very little "give" and if you want to catch garfish the expense is justified. We have done well with Damyl Imperial Steelpower and Platil Strong.

Hooks

The choice of the correct hook is of the greatest importance when fishing for garfish. A garfish has a long, beak-like mouth and a wrongly chosen hook will not easily hold in such a mouth. If the hook is too large, the point will settle outside the mouth when the garfish takes – and the fish cannot be hooked. If, on the other hand, the hook is too small, it will just miss the piece of soft tissue in the mouth. We have tested a large number of hooks and can recommend two. Personally we prefer the first, a blade-end hook. The second has a small eye.

A. Mustad Kendal Round Qual. 1253 A, hook no. 6.
B. Mustad Beak Qual. 92259, hook no. 8 or 9.

Ask your dealer for these two hooks and if necessary get him to order them for you.

The Stabilo float

The Stabilo float is the result of years of effort to develop a sea float which can be cast a very long distance. The secret of this patented float lies in the shape which gradually changes from round to square, making the float very stable during its passage through the air. For garfish it is not always necessary to fish far from the shore, but when it is essential, the Stabilo will cover 70–80m if required. The float is entirely hand-made and is available in weights of 15 (½), 30 (1), 50 (2) and 70g (2½oz). It has a body of dense and heavy cork, unlike a number of inferior imitations which are made of polystyrene, balsa wood or pressed cork.
When fishing in places where long-distance casting is not essential, you could opt for the cheaper alternatives, such as bubble floats or long hollow plastic floats.

Float colour

Most floats have a bright orange tip to make them visible from a distance. But garfish are not stupid, and in places where large numbers of anglers are after them, the presence of the coloured floats will be seen as a danger signal. We would therefore advise you to give at least one of your floats an inconspicuous camouflage colour. Most float bodies are green and can be left untouched. The orange tip should be painted dull black and the black paint then spread over the green part with a cloth, so that the black runs into the green. The float will now resemble a piece of wood.

Bait

The most popular bait for garfish is a strip cut from the tail of a previously caught specimen. It is an effective bait, which is, moreover, firmly held on the hook during casting. However, it must be repeatedly renewed. The fresher the better.
Fresh sandeel also makes an excellent bait, but does not stay on the hook very well. A sandeel may save the day even when a garfish patch has been fished practically bare. Early in the season the garfish will take a boiled shrimp, too. Finally, some garfish are tempted by ragworm, lugworm and even earthworms.

Fresh sandeels make an excellent garfish bait

Strip of fish used for catching garfish

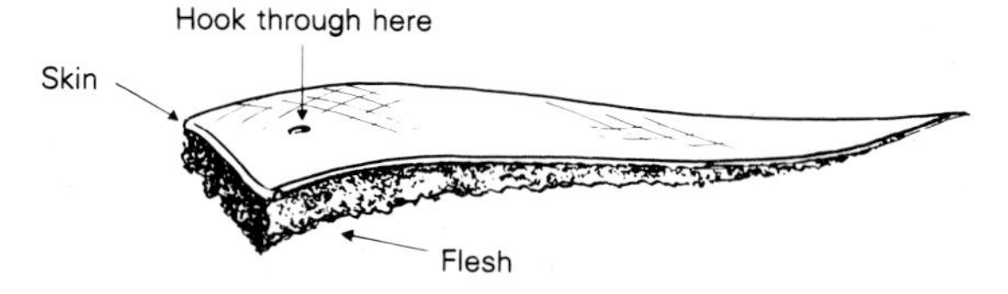

Fixing the trace to the sea float

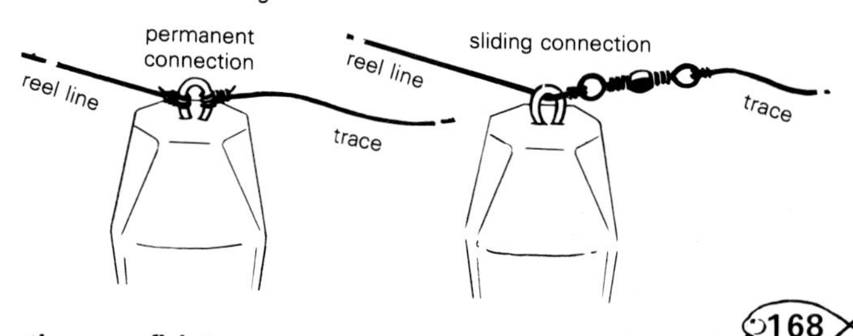

168

Mounting a garfish trace

Both reel line and trace must be tied to the tip of the float; this will avoid them becoming entangled. Strange but true! When the garfish takes, the float will not be pulled down but *up*. From a distance this waterski effect is particularly noticeable.
An angling colleague developed another method, passing the reel line through the metal eyelet ring of the float and then tying it to a small swivel or a split ring, to which the trace is also attached. When taking the bait, the garfish pulls the reel line through the eyelet and the bite is immediately felt at the rod tip. A very sensitive method of fishing.
The minimum length of a trace should be 1 metre, but 1.50m is better. Since the garfish's very sharp teeth will damage the trace just above the hook, we recommend that the trace be replaced after every fifth fish caught, otherwise it will break at an unforeseen moment.

A good garfish mark (see tip 170)

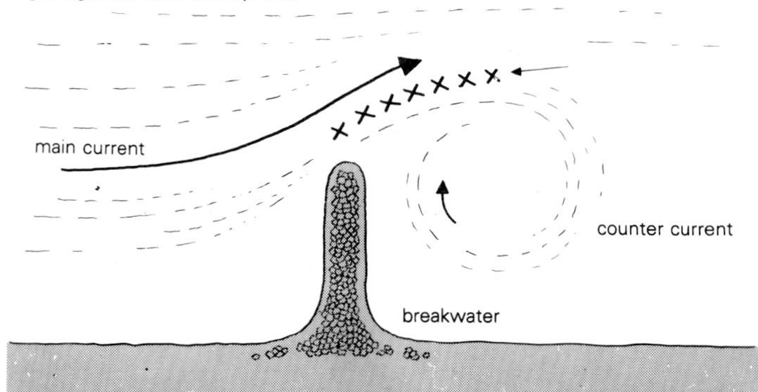

Technique of fishing for garfish

If you should ever be fortunate enough to find yourself the only angler at a known garfish mark, try to remain far enough from the water's edge to induce the shy garfish to feed close to the shore. You will then not have to cast over a great distance. When you are fishing with several other anglers, you will inevitably be forced to cast far out to sea. Try to cast beyond the fish then carefully draw the bait back towards them. Pay attention! Just before the bite occurs you will frequently see the tail of a rising garfish just behind the bait. It happens only for a moment and is the finest and most exciting experience imaginable. You know that the garfish is close to the bait – will he take it? Leave it for about ten seconds before slowly pulling it towards you. The disappearing bait may stimulate the fish to take after all.
When you have caught a garfish, hold it by the middle and wait until it has stopped flapping. If you want to keep it, kill the fish immediately by hitting it on the head. The hook can then be removed.

Garfish grounds

Good garfish marks are found wherever the current runs over shallow submerged breakwaters. Remember where you have been successful in the past, for garfish have a pronounced preference for certain spots. What has been a good garfish mark once will always remain so. If you want to fish for garfish from the beach, try to find the dividing line between the main current and the returning counter current (see sketch). This is where garfish tend to congregate. When fishing from the beach the first few hours of an incoming tide will present the best opportunities. When fishing from a breakwater or groyne continue to fish throughout the tide, but the clear water at the turn of the tide is the best time of all.
The best times of the day are the first few hours after sunrise and at dusk.

29. MACKEREL AND SHAD

171

Mackerel fishing from large charter boats

Mackerel fishing from large charter boats is a popular branch of sea fishing. Whether it is the most attractive is something else! It is in any case not difficult and for that reason mackerel fishing constitutes an easy introduction to sea fishing. We therefore gladly take this opportunity to provide some good advice about this branch of fishing also, in the hope that the primitive method of hoisting mackerel from the sea will awaken the reader's interest in more attractive ways of fishing.

To begin with pick a good spot on the boat, preferably near the wheelhouse. The best place of all is the bow, where no-one will bother you. The firm boat rod must be solid enough to deal with a pound of lead and seven pounds of thrashing mackerel. Such a rod requires a strong reel, loaded with braided Terylene with a capacity of 20 to 30lb. A three to seven-hook feather paternoster is tied to the line. With a three-hook paternoster you can catch three mackerel at once, and with a seven-hook one . . . who knows? Let's stick to a three-hook specimen. A 300g (11oz) lead is attached to the bottom end. It has to be heavy enough not to drift sideways into your neighbour's line. If necessary even heavier lead can be used. The whole thing is allowed to sink rapidly. As soon as the lead touches bottom the line is slowly wound in. While doing so, you regularly flick your rod tip, so that the paternoster keeps moving. As soon as you feel a take strike immediately and wind in the fish.

By the way: please do not take more fish than you can eat. A correctly unhooked mackerel *can* be put back.

Catching mackerel and shad from a small boat

That is indeed another story. In fishing for mackerel and shad from a small boat you will discover what excellent sport these two fish can provide – on condition that appropriate equipment is used. The equipment might consist of a spinning rod with a lightweight reel loaded with 7lb line. A small jig is tied to the line. It is cast towards the spot where screeching seagulls are diving to feast on the small fish driven to the surface by mackerel and shad. It is then recovered with short jerks. The speed of recovery determines the level at which the jig moves through the water. You will have to discover how deep the fish are swimming. Shad (a large predatory herring) usually swim in the surface layers, while mackerel and horse mackerel are found somewhat deeper in the water.

173

Mackerel and shad fishing from the shore

In autumn it sometimes happens that large flocks of squawking seagulls are diving close to the shore. This may indicate the presence of shoals of mackerel or shad hunting for sprats. At such times you might try to cast a jig or a heavy spoon among the feeding fish, using a long casting rod. If that does not work, a Pirk might do the trick, for such a lure can be cast over great distances. The most recent solution to the distance problem is provided by the Stabilo float, with which maximum casts of about 100m may be achieved. A trace, approximately a metre in length, with a hook and a piece of fish, is tied to the top of the float. The float is cast and is then slowly drawn in. As at such a distance it is very difficult to set the hook correctly, it is necessary to strike firmly several times when the fish has taken the bait. This method of fishing can present the angler with great surprises. Among other fish we have caught turbot, a very large flounder, a giant eel and a 5lb bass in this way!

Fly-fishing for mackerel and shad!

We never let an opportunity of fly-fishing for sea fish go by. On many occasions we have been terribly clumsy and bungled the operation, but now we know exactly when it can be done and when it will fail. We always carry our fly rods on board and wait patiently for the chance to use them. Essential conditions are: the absence of current and wind and the presence of feeding fish in clear water. When conditions are favourable we exult in catching mackerel and shad on our fly rods. You cannot imagine the enjoyment! And what sporting fish they are – we never before suspected that shad could make such tremendous leaps. Each time we look forward with pleasure to the next occasion. Unfortunately the opportunity does not arise often enough.

30. COD AND CODLING

Cod and codling fishing

Cod are by far the largest fish caught regularly in our coastal waters. Only the stingray is heavier, but the average angler's chances of catching cod are a thousand times higher. The record cod was caught by a beginner and weighed 53lb! It is not surprising that legions of anglers are addicted to cod and codling fishing. The smaller fish, up to 6lb, are called codling; everything above that weight is proudly referred to as a cod. We modestly fish for codling, secretly hoping to catch cod. The codling season runs from October to April and codling fishing is therefore essentially an occupation for the hardy winter angler.
Codling and cod like deep water, but are occasionally tempted to shallower water by the rich food supplies near jetties, piers and submerged breakwaters.
Experienced anglers know from experience that far more codling and cod are caught at night than during the daytime. It appears to have something to do with the nightly trek of large shoals of shrimps towards the shore.

A beautifully marked 18lb cod caught on a flexible nylon trace

Cod grounds

Piers and parts of the beach lit at night by dozens of large and small lights indicate good cod grounds. This additional coastal lighting is produced by the small army of anglers who, with dripping noses, practise their beloved sport shoulder to shoulder. If you have no wish to spend your leisure time having to use your elbows, you should try to find alternative patches by inquiring locally or by studying a good map. Look for deep gullies within casting distance of the shore. If there are no deep gullies parallel to the beach, look out for one at right angles, usually noticeable at low tide. As a rule such gullies abound with fish. Strong currents have worn out deep channels to either side of jetties. As a rule these provide excellent fishing grounds, though unfortunately they are difficult to reach from the shore so the ability to cast a long way is essential.

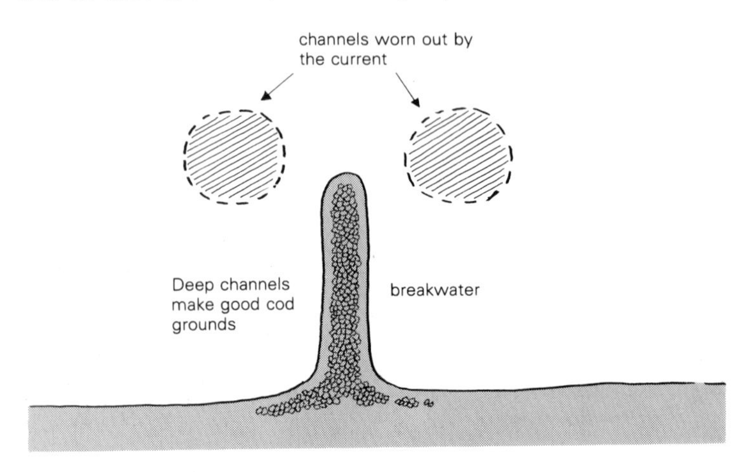

The effect of tides on cod catches

Beach anglers like to fish for cod in the period just before and after low tide. This is in the first place because the deep gullies are easy to fish at low tides and in the second place because at that time the speed of the current is relatively low.
Cod anglers who fish from piers can catch fish at any state of the tide. In addition there are a growing number of cod anglers who specialise in fishing at high tide. They often wade out far into the water and cast fine lines over great distances. Their results confirm our opinion that cod can be caught whatever the state of the tide. From conversations with professional fishermen we have learnt that shoals of cod adapt their routes to the tides. Although cod feed at any time, the presence of fish in certain grounds depends on the tide.
You should therefore analyse your cod catches (and those of other anglers) from a certain patch and draw your conclusions accordingly. Go fishing at times which have proved to be favourable for cod fishing in the past. But maintain your vigilance!

Bait

Lugworm is the most popular bait for cod fishing. Not because it is the best bait, but because it is the most readily available. When you fish with lugworm, follow our advice and gut the worms before threading them on the hook (see tip 66). Worms treated in this way stay more firmly on the hook and withstand the force of the cast very well. We guarantee that they remain equally effective.
The very best bait for cod fishing is the extra large lugworm imported from France (see tip 68). It has a pronounced scent, irresistible to codling and cod. A fresh worm is very tough and stays firmly on the hook. Deep-frozen worms are also effective, provided they have been carefully thawed.
If you are short of bait there is no reason why you should not augment the lugworm with mussels, shrimps, sprats, smelts or strips of fish, for codling will swallow anything that looks or smells edible.

Cod traces

The times at which you fish for cod dictate that the possibilities of catching other fish are remote. The size of the hook (4/0) ensures that nothing but the largest whiting could take the bait away, so you might just as well make up your trace with no reservations for other species, except . . . Cod do feed on whiting, and though it is not possible to cast a whiting any appreciable distance, you might like to try the following: above the snood with the lugworm baited 4/0 tie a second snood equipped with a smaller hook – about size 1. Bait this hook with lugworm and hopefully it will be taken by a whiting. The whiting may then be taken by a cod along with the 4/0. Even if the whiting is not taken it should provide an added attractor to the 4/0. If a cod doesn't come along you have at least caught a whiting!

The Breakaway lead in cod fishing

The Breakaway lead was designed for fishing shallow water either from a boat or from the shore. Basically it is an improvement on the grapnel lead. The wires are not set solidly into the lead, but locked into position by locating plastic beads in grooves which run along the torpedo-shaped lead. When a fish takes the bait and pulls away, the beads pop out of the grooves and the wires collapse to trail limply behind the lead.
The leads are used extensively along the Thames estuary for cod, skate and stingray. If you have difficulty obtaining them, write direct to Breakaway Tackle, Ipswich, Suffolk. The leads are an integral part of boatcasting, which is described in Tip 184.

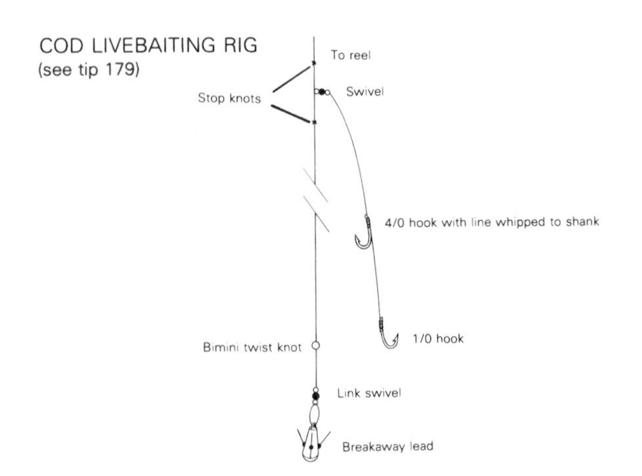

The imposing head of a 23lb cod

Whiting

Our friend the cod belongs to a very large family and some of its relations which closely resemble it are found in coastal waters as well: the pout, the coalfish and the pollack, to mention but a few. Whiting are found in large numbers all around our coast. A pity that this cod-like fish does not grow very large: a 3lb whiting is

quite a good specimen. At times the fishing grounds are so crowded with whiting that it is impossible to catch anything else. At such times remember the legal minimum size for whiting: 25cm (9½in).
As a rule the whiting is found at higher levels in the water than its relations. If you want to catch this fish you are advised to tie at least one snood at a considerable distance above the lead.

Cod fishing from a boat

The success of cod fishing from a large charter boat depends entirely on your fellow passengers. If everybody uses heavy grapnel leads, the results may be quite favourable, but woe betide if there are a few jokers on board who are fishing with lightweight lead. In that case most of the day will be spent in disentangling lines.
Cod fishing from a small boat with only two anglers on board is an entirely different matter. Four rods can be used at once, two at the stern with smooth boat lead and two sideways with very heavy grapnel leads. Allow it to anchor safely before tightening the line. When a fish takes, carefully tighten the line and strike. If no resistance is felt the rod is laid down again, but if you experience contact with the fish, strike again firmly, twice.

Artificial bait for cod?

Anglers all over Europe gratefully exploit the knowledge that cod will take anything that moves in its neighbourhood. Plenty of cod and codling are caught on heavy chrome-plated pirks sometimes made from the door handles of cars and lorries or lengths of heavy tube.
Cod fans fishing in coastal waters, however, are deeply distressed if they are unable to obtain lugworms or ragworms. Why is artificial bait not used in the North Sea? Because it is thought that the concentration of fish is too low to make this method successful. And also because it is thought that visibility in the muddy coastal waters is so bad that the cod uses senses other than sight to obtain its food. Nevertheless, we have arranged with a number of anglers keen to experiment that when conditions are favourable (clear water during a slack tide), we shall seriously try to fish for cod with artificial bait. You are herewith invited to take part in the experiment. We shall be glad to learn of your experiences.

31. BASS

One of the largest bass ever caught in Dutch waters (length 80cm – 31½in)

The bass

The bass is the nearest we can hope to get to finding the perfect fish. It can be caught by a variety of methods, fights well, is attractive and pleasing to the eye and, finally, tastes good!

The methods which can be used to take bass are governed by the weather. In early June when thousands of crabs are peeling their shells, bass are often within feet of the shore, running along the gullies and channels with the flooding tide. Off steep shingle beaches, they'll often come up the beach with a wave while chasing sandeels; obviously the Redgill can be put to good effect here.

Besides water temperature and the availability of food, the next most important factor which governs the bass's mode of feeding is water clarity. In clear water bass can be taken (and hectic sport is to be had) with spinners and spoons. Often long casting is unnecessary. School bass can be terrific sport on fly tackle and streamer lures, fished in the clear mouths of rivers where they enter the sea.

Where to catch bass

Close to the shore bass may be expected in places where strong currents meet obstacles such as jetties and submerged breakwaters. From the shelter of a shallow bank or a counter-current the bass keeps its eye on everything carried along by the current. As soon as a small fish or a crab comes within its field of vision it instantly pounces on its prey. However, bass only forage in this manner in clear water. As soon as the water becomes murky the fish leave these "observation posts" and move towards the beaches, where they can be caught in the immediate neighbourhood of outcrops of rocks, piers, groynes, etc especially at high tide. If you want to catch bass from the beach, this is where and when your chances will be best.
In the open sea, bass also have their favourite grounds. We have found that the fish often feed in the calm water close to the tide-race which occurs when the current hits a shallow sandbank. Such a spot is not without danger to the boat angler, for nothing is more treacherous than a tide-race. It would be better to cast a long way rather than venture too close to one.

Bass waiting behind an obstacle

186

Catching bass from the shore

If you want to catch bass from the shore, your bait should preferably consist of ragworm or crab. Mount one or two hooks, size 2/0 or 1/0 and fish a flowing trace on a running paternoster. Cast close to groynes, piers or rocks – the closer the better – and wind in very slowly, at a speed of 3 metres a minute. This active method of fishing will yield the best results. It also minimises the bother of crabs, although crabs do little harm to your bait. On the contrary, a reasonably sized bass will effortlessly swallow your bait, *and* the crab. How far should the bait be wound in? Although we have never caught a bass close to the beach we would still advise you to retrieve the bait right into the shadows for bass have been seen harrying small fish in water too shallow to cover them completely.
Be extremely careful when you pick up a bass. It has vicious spiney fins which can cause nasty wounds. Draw the fish on to the beach and hold it in a wet cloth while you unhook it.

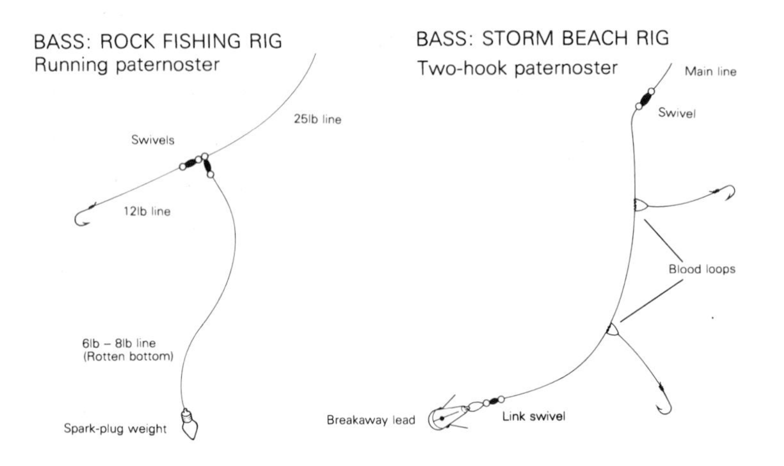

187

Which natural bait for bass?

We dutifully investigate the stomach contents of all the bass we kill for the table. In bass caught over submerged breakwaters we have found a stomach content of 70 per cent crab, 20 per cent small fish and ten per cent shrimp. On the other hand the stomach contents of fish caught over a sandy bottom consisted mainly of shrimp: 50 per cent, with 40 per cent crab and ten per cent small fish. On average, crab is thus seen to form the largest part of a bass's diet. We have alternated the well-known baits like ragworm and lugworm with crab, shrimp and small fish. Can you guess which of these yielded the best results? Yes indeed, it was the ragworm. Crab, both hard and soft, came a close second. We used small crabs which were fixed on the hook with rubber bands. When we discovered that bass make no distinction between hard and soft crab, we stopped looking for the latter. Hard crabs are plentiful and we are no longer bothered by small fish. When using ragworm it is advisable to bait up with one very large one.

Artificial bait

When fishing from jetties, piers or rocks you could try for bass with heavy spinners, spoons or jigs. You may expect to lose plenty of artificials, for to be successful you will have to fish close to these features, and this is risky. It is much easier to fish for bass with artificial lures from a boat. The best artificial bait is a red and white feather paternoster which is moved up and down close to the bottom from a boat drifting in the current. On good bass marks the speed of the current is usually so great that spoon and jigs do not get deep enough, whereas a heavily leaded feather paternoster copes quite well with a strong current. However, shoals of shad and mackerel, which often swim above bass, may prevent the feather paternoster reaching the appropriate level. In that case you should either use extra heavy lead, or sink the paternoster at some distance in front of the hot-spot and wait until the current takes it to the correct point.

The technique of fishing with a feather paternoster

Many anglers make the mistake of jerking the bass paternoster up and down too far and too fast. However attractive the flash of the feathers, the bass will then not take them when they are fished like this.
Move the bait up and down with small jerks if you want to increase your chances of catching bass. Strike as fast as possible at every take, for the fish will quickly reject the feathers when it finds out its mistake. Remember that a slackening of the line may also indicate a take. It is easier to strike with a stiff rod than with too flexible a rod. Since ordinary fishing line has too much "give", we prefer to use a 20 or 30lb braided Terylene line. This non-stretch line makes it easier to set the hook; the movements of the feather paternoster are more easily controlled and a snagged hook can be straightened if necessary.

Special feather paternosters for bass

The feather paternoster sold for mackerel fishing and other fish are nearly all unsuitable for bass. As a rule the hooks are too small; the knots are frequently unreliable, the snoods too long and the number of hooks too large. We would therefore strongly advise you to tie your own. It really is not all that difficult. We make ours from 38lb line with 3 or 4 very short sidelines. We tie one red and four white feathers to each hook. Experiments conducted over a long period have proved that this combination of red and white is the most effective in all conditions. The numbers of fish we have caught on these red and white feathers are many.
The hooks must be large and strong enough to hold a good-sized fish, but on the other hand they should be flexible enough to be straightened with a 30lb braided sea line when they become snagged. The Mustad Limerick Hook Qual. 7813 B no. 3/0 is an excellent hook.

32. MULLET

191

Mullet

The mullet is a fantastic game fish, difficult to catch and incredibly strong. After he had played his first thick-lipped mullet our friend, the well-known Dutch angler Kees Ketter, who has caught more salmon than anyone else we know, declared – panting with emotion – that the mullet is a much more vigorous fighter than the salmon.
About 12 years ago we caught a large mullet on a streamer, then, soon after, a second and a third. We started to think deeply about the species, to observe and to experiment, and the fish gradually began to shed its mysteries. We have now reached a stage where we regularly make large catches of mullet. We know approximately where to fish, at what states of the tide; we use the correct equipment and the correct bait. For all that is very important.

Three kinds of mullet

For the sake of convenience we speak of "mullet", but three species occurring in our waters should be distinguished, namely
the thin-lipped mullet (*Mugil capito*)
the thick-lipped mullet (*Mugil labrosus*)
the golden-grey mullet (*Mugil auratus*)
They are easy to distinguish; the names speak for themselves. If the mullet you have caught does not have a thick, callous upper lip, it is a thin-lipped mullet. It's as simple as that. Golden-grey mullet have a golden spot on each gill cover.
The three species occur separately as well as in mixed shoals, but often differ in behaviour and feeding habits.

The photograph shows the protuberances covering the lip of the thick-lipped mullet

Where to find mullet

193

Mullet are found
a. In the mouth of rivers, canals, deltas and enclosed estuaries, where the fish enters and leaves via the locks.
b. In practically all sea harbours.
c. Near dykes, submerged breakwaters and jetties.

Mullet, mainly the thin-lipped variety, often swim some distance up rivers and canals. All harbours have a permanent mullet population, which roams the harbour according to a fixed pattern, taking pot luck so far as their food is concerned. Mullet feeding near dykes, jetties and submerged breakwaters are mainly of the thick-lipped variety. Their feeding pattern is determined by the tide. An angler who succeeds in discovering their timetable will know when and where to fish.

Urban mullet and wild mullet

Mullet can be further divided into two groups: urban mullet and wild mullet. Urban mullet is the fish which, so far as behaviour and feeding are concerned, has adapted itself entirely to the presence of man and to the food available. It is possible to persuade the mullet to take a certain bait, for instance bread, by feeding it over a period of time.

Wild mullet feed on tiny organisms living in the mud and on musselbanks. We have often caught mullet with stomachs full of mussel brood. However, as a rule the contents of a mullet's stomach are unrecognisable. Wild mullet can be tempted to take streamers and feather paternosters; as a rule these are thick-lipped mullet. They can also, on occasions, be weaned on to bread baits. Thin lips in rivers take small harbour ragworms avidly.

195

Which bait for urban mullet?

The best bait for urban mullet is that which naturally forms part of their daily diet. In other words, mussels for mullet living in mussel harbours and fish refuse in fishing harbours. Roe also makes an excellent bait. So good, in fact, that we suspect mullet to be roe poachers of the first order. We have occasionally had success with a paste made from the contents of a mullet's stomach and we have also had good catches with pieces of fresh fish liver. And even with bread, after extensive pre-baiting.

We are not very keen on the use of pieces of seaweed, algae and lettuce. A mullet's stomach occasionally contains green substances, but we do not believe that the fish actually forages for this type of food. It sometimes enters its stomach when the fish is sucking seaweed. We have often observed mullet pulling the growth off the bottom, off posts and rocks, to eat the tiny creatures living on it. In shallow water the fish frequently stand on their heads while doing so, their mighty tails flapping above the water. When you see this phenomenon there is no doubt that you are watching mullet.

Behaviour of wild mullet

The wild mullet behaves in a much more aggressive manner than the urban mullet. We suspect that this is due to the large shoals of small fish which forage in the same places and for the same food as the mullet. Possibly it is envy and jealousy which makes the large fish pounce upon their small competitors. We can find no other explanation for the fact that we get such tremendous takes when using streamers – which imitate small fish – or paternoster flies. Investigations into the contents of mullet stomachs have shown that they literally never include small fish or fish remains (recognisable from the scales). On the other hand the stomachs of mullet caught on streamers were often filled to capacity with mussel brood. Are you still with us? The point is that mullet can be caught with artificial bait. We have found that green and green/white streamers are by far the most effective for catching mullet, the former being favourite one day, the green/white combination yielding better results at other times. Our mullet paternosters therefore incorporate both.

Fishing for urban mullet

A match rod can be used when fishing from the shore, but an Avon, carp or light pike rod will also do. A float may be used to keep the bait at a certain depth, but when the fish is very shy, float and lead should be dispensed with in order to allow the bait to flutter down in the most natural manner possible.

We recommend a line of maximum 7lb, in the pious hope that a hooked mullet will not swim round a post. On a thicker line you will get fewer bites. The hook must be small but strong. The hooks recommended for garfish are very effective (see tip 164).

Fish close to or on the bottom. Make sure that you have a very large landing net to hand. Mullet are a very rigid fish and must be scooped up in one go. If you should accidentally touch the fish with the edge of the net you can as a rule say goodbye to it.

Fishing for wild mullet

If you want to fish for wild mullet with a feather paternoster, you should preferably use a short casting rod with a stiff tip. Such a rod will best enable you to control the movements of the paternoster and to react faster to a take. The fishing line should be at least 18lb, or even thicker when you are fishing from a height and the fish has to be lifted on the line. Personally we like to use braided Terylene. Lower the paternoster close to posts, walls or rocks, until the lead touches bottom. Now move the feathers up and down with short jerks. It is a mistake to haul the tackle wildly up and down: the fish will have no chance to take the feathers. As soon as you feel a peculiar rasping bite you must strike immediately. Also strike when you suddenly miss the weight of the lead for this also indicates a take. Immediate striking is essential, for the mullet will quickly let go when it realises its mistake. You may take it from us that if you catch one fish to every two takes you are a champion mullet catcher. Thin-lipped mullet very often live in the lower reaches of rivers, moving up and down with the tide, and can be caught on floatfished harbour ragworm.

Groundbaiting

Mullet may be lured to a certain patch by means of groundbaiting. Urban mullet, in particular, often respond very well to groundbaiting and it is even possible to induce mullet to start feeding when they are apparently idly swimming about. In fact, groundbaiting may cause a veritable frenzy of feeding and the angler who is able to create such a phenomenon is in a very favourable position and may be able to take one mullet after another. Groundbait for urban mullet may consist of a basis of bread, combined with fish offal or squashed fish, pieces of seaweed, mussels and roe. For wild mullet we always use crushed mussels though they can be induced to take bread by groundbaiting. We lay down a layer and from time to time throw in a few additional mussels while we are fishing. When you are fishing alone you should groundbait two swims and fish them alternatively. When you have disturbed one swim by playing a mullet, you immediately switch over to the other. If you have groundbaited only one patch, add some fresh groundbait immediately after each strike.

Special mullet paternoster

No doubt there is a demand for one, for when mackerel feather rigs have been used for mullet fishing they have often proved to be disappointing. When mullet take the feathers, many of them are lost either because of incorrect hooks or because the knots do not stand up to the vigorous resistance of the fish. Naturally, you can make your own paternosters; it is not at all difficult. Use 38lb line and tie green and green/white feathers to very short snoods – three are more than enough. We recommend Mustad Round Bend Sea Hooks Qual. 2315 no. 10. (For constructing paternosters also see tip 75).
In conclusion we wish you many exciting adventures at sea.

Ivan and Igor Garay